On the Firing Line

(Anna Chapin Ray and Hamilton Brock Fuller)

CHAPTER ONE

Six feet one in his stockings, broad-shouldered and without an ounce of extra flesh, Harvard Weldon suddenly halted before one of a line of deck chairs.

"I usually get what I want, Miss Dent," he observed suggestively.

"You are more fortunate than most people." Her answering tone was dry.

Most men would have been baffled by her apparent indifference. Not so was Weldon. Secure in the possession of a good tailor and an equally good digestion, he was willing to await the leisurely course of events.

"My doctor always advises mild exercise after lunch," he continued.

"You are in the care of a physician?" she queried, with a whimsical glance up at his brown face and athletic figure.

"Not just now. I was once, however." She raised her brows in polite interrogation. Her involuntary thawing of a moment before had given place to absolute conventionality. Weldon smiled to himself, as he noted the change. He had been at sea for three days now, and those three days had been chiefly spent in trying to penetrate the social shell of his next neighbor at table. It was not so much that Ethel Dent was undeniably pretty as that he had been piqued by her frosty reception of his efforts to supplement the services of a careless waiter.

Now, uninvited, he dropped into the empty chair next her own.

"If I may?" he said questioningly, as he raised his cap. "Yes, I have had a doctor twice. Once was measles, once a collar bone broken in football. Both times, I was urged to take a walk after luncheon. Is Miss Arthur--?"

He hesitated for the right word. Still ignoring his obvious hint, Ethel Dent supplied the word, without charity for her luckless chaperon. "Horridly seasick." She pointed out to the level steely- gray sea. "And on this duck-pond," she added.

Her accent was expressive. Weldon laughed.

"Perhaps she isn't as used to the duck-pond as you are."

The girl brushed a lock of vivid gold hair from her eyes; then she sat up, to add emphasis to her words. "Miss Arthur has been to America and back seven times and to Australia once," she said conclusively.

"As globe-trotter, or as commercial traveller?"

"Neither. As professional chaperon. When she applied for me, she stated--" The girl caught her breath and stopped short.

"Well?" he asked encouragingly. She shook her head. Again, for an instant, Weldon could see the humanity beneath the veneering. Moreover, he liked what he saw. The blue eyes were honest and steady. One mocking dimple belied the gravity of the firm lips.

"What did she state?" he asked again.

"It's not manners to tell tales about one's companion," she demurred.

"Not if you spell it with a little c. With a capital, it becomes professional, and you can say what you choose. Miss Arthur is a righteous lady; nevertheless, she is a bit professional. And you were saying that the lady stated--"

"That she never had been seasick in her life."

"Oh. And did she also produce certificates as to her moral character? Or is fibbing merely bad form nowadays?"

With swift inconsequence, the girl shifted to the other side of the discussion.

"Of course, this may be a first attack."

"Of course," Weldon assented gravely. But again she shifted her ground. "Only," she continued, with her eyes thoughtfully fixed on the distant, impersonal point where sea and sky met; "only it is a little strange that, yesterday, I heard her tell the stewardess she never took beeftea when she was seasick."

"Oh." Weldon's eyes joined hers on the sky-line. "I have heard of similar cases before."

"She offered to come on deck," Ethel went on quietly. "It was generous of her, for she knew I was left entirely alone. Nevertheless, I persuaded her that she was better off in her berth."

Leaning back in the chair of the absent invalid, Weldon watched his companion out of the corners of his eyes and rejoiced at the change in her. Even while he rejoiced, he marvelled. A Canadian by birth and education, he had rarely come in contact with English girls. At first, he had been totally at a loss to account for the haughty chill in the manner of this one. Grown accustomed to that, he was still more at a loss to account for this sudden awakening into humanity. He had as yet to learn that two days of having her only companion seasick, coupled with a sparkling sun and a crisp breeze, can rouse even a duenna-led English girl to the point of expressing her opinions pithily and with vigor.

As the Dunottar Castle had slid away from Southampton, three days before, Weldon had tramped briskly up and down the crowded deck, taking mental note of his companions for the next two weeks. Among the caped and capped throng leaning over the rail and staring after the receding shore with homesick eyes, he saw little to interest him. Neither did the shore interest him in the least. His own partings had come, two weeks before, when the steam yacht had put back from Sandy Hook. Now, accordingly, he went in search of the dining-room steward to whom he gave much gold and instruction. Then he betook himself to his stateroom where his mates were already busy settling their belongings.

The luncheon hour disclosed the fact that the dining-room steward had earned his money and had digested his instruction. A short pause on the threshold informed Weldon that the Dunottar Castle held exactly one pretty girl; the steward informed Weldon that the vacant chair beside her was his own. Weldon picked up his napkin with a brief prayer of thanksgiving. What if he was going out to Africa in search of Boers and glory? There was no especial reason he should not enjoy himself on the way.

Weldon had gained a wide experience of American girls. well-bred, well-chaperoned, nevertheless they offered possible points of contact to the strangers with whom they were thrown. To all seeming, Ethel Dent was as accessible as the outer wall of an ice palace. Beside her decorous ignoring of his existence, Miss Arthur, lean and spectacled and sniffy, appeared to be of maternal kindliness, albeit her only advances had been a muffled request for the salt. The next morning, Miss Arthur's chair had been empty, and her charge, left to herself, had been more glacially circumspect than ever. Whatever skittish traits the pair might develop, Weldon felt assured that they would be solely upon the side of Miss Ophelia Arthur.

Now, however, he was giving himself praise for his own astute generalship. It was no slight matter, at the end of the third day, to find himself sitting next to Miss Dent in the line of steamer chairs and even bending over to pick up the novel she had dropped. In his elation, Weldon neglected to give credit to Miss Arthur whose digestive woes were the cause of the whole situation. Only the riper Christianity which comes with declining years can make one wholly loyal to a seasick comrade.

He gave himself yet more praise, next morning at sunrise, when he found himself pacing the deck at Ethel Dent's side. As a rule, he and his mates rose betimes and, clad in slippers and pajamas, raced up and down the decks to keep their muscles in hard order, before descending for the tubbing which is the matin duty of every self- respecting British subject. This morning, instead of the deserted decks and the pajama-clad athletes, the passengers were out early to catch the first glimpse of Madeira, and Weldon, starchy and glowing with much cold water, was on deck to catch the first glimpse of Ethel.

Miss Arthur was still invisible, and the girl was discreetly late about appearing. The deck was full, when at last she came in sight; and it seemed, to her first glance, that she was the only unattended person abroad, that morning. Her chin rose a little aggressively as she moved forward. Then her eyes lighted. Cap in hand, Weldon stood in her direct path.

"Good morning," he said. "We've just passed the lighthouse and are nearly opposite Canical. If you come over here, you can see it."

His tone was matter-of-course, yet masterful. At the very beginning of her fourth solitary day, Ethel admitted to herself that it was good to have some one take possession of her in this summary fashion.

"Is Miss Arthur still unhappy?" he asked, as he swung into step at her side.

"Yes. She has taken to her hymnal, this morning, in search of consolation. I tried to coax her to get up and go ashore; but she said there was no use in experiencing the same woe twice."

"I am afraid I do not quite catch the lady's line of argument," Weldon remarked doubtfully.

The girl laughed. Then she decorously checked her laugh and endeavored to turn sympathetic once more.

"She means to make one prolonged illness. Else she will only recover in order to fall ill again." "Oh." Weldon's tone was still blank. "And shall you go ashore?"

She shook her head.

"I am sorry. You would find any amount to see."

"I am sorry, too," she said frankly. "Still, I don't see how I can, without Miss Arthur."

His hands in his pockets, Weldon took a dozen steps in doubtful silence.

"I'll tell you what we can do, Miss Dent: Harry Carew, one of the fellows going out with me, had a note of introduction to Colonel Scott and his wife. He is the pompous old Englishman across the table. I'll get Carew to introduce us, and perhaps they will let us go ashore with them."

"But are they going?" she asked irresolutely.

"Surely. We have three hours here. I know Carew's mother well; she and Mrs. Scott were schoolmates at Madame Prather's in London."

She looked up with sudden interest.

"Madame Prather's? That is where I have been, for the past five years."

"Then we are all right," Weldon said coolly. "The arrangement is made. Carew is the only missing link. Excuse me, and I will go in search of him."

It was high noon when the Dunottar Castle finally weighed anchor at Funchal and started on her long, unbroken voyage to the southward. Side by side in the stern, Weldon and Ethel looked back at the blue harbor dotted with the myriad little boats, at the quaint town backed with its amphitheatre of sunlit hills and, poised on the summit, the church where Nossa Senhora do Monte keeps watch and ward over the town beneath. Ethel's experience was the broader for her hilarious ride in a bullock-drawn palanquin. Weldon's experience was more instructive. It taught him that, her hat awry and her yellow hair loosened about her laughing face, Ethel Dent was tenfold more attractive than when she made her usual decorous entrance to the dining-room.

Mrs. Scott had been a willing chaperon and an efficient one. Nevertheless, as they stood together in the stern, looking out across the gold-flecked sea,

Weldon felt that he had made a long stride, that morning, towards acquaintance with his companion. And, even now, the voyage was nearly all before them.

As if in answer to his thoughts, she lifted her eyes to his face.

"Twelve more days!" she said slowly.

"Are you sorry?"

She shook her head.

"Glad and sorry both. I love the sea; but home is at the end of it."

"You live out there?" he asked.

She smiled at the question. "Yes, if out there means Cape Town. At least, my parents live there."

"How long have you been in England?" he queried, while, abandoning all pretence of interest in the fast-vanishing town, he turned his back to the rail in order to face his companion more directly.

"Always, except for one year, six years ago, and a summer--summer in England, I mean--two years later."

Rather inconsequently, Weldon attacked the side issue suggested by her words.

"How does it seem to have one's seasons standing on their heads?"

She answered question with question. "Haven't you been out before?"

"No."

"I supposed you had taken the voyage any number of times. But about the seasons, it doesn't count for much until you come to Christmas. No England-born mortal can hang up his stocking in mid-summer without a pang of regretful homesickness."

Weldon laughed.

"Do you substitute a refrigerator for a chimney corner?" he asked. "But are you England-born?"

"Yes. My father went out only seven years ago. The 'home' tradition is so strong that I was sent back to school and for a year of social life. My little brother goes to Harrow in two years. Even in Cape Town, a few people still hold true to the tradition of the public school."

Weldon nodded assent.

"We meet it in Canada, now and then; not too often, though. So in reality you are almost as much a stranger to Cape Town as I am."

"Quite. My father says it is all changed now. It used to be a lazy little place; now it is pandemonium, soldiers and supplies going out, time-expired men and invalids coming in. Mr. Weldon--"

His questioning smile answered the pause in her sentence.

"Well?" he asked, after a prolonged interval.

Her teeth shut on her lower lip, she stared at the wide blue sea with wide blue eyes. Something in its restless tossing, in the changing lights that darted back to her from the crests of the waves, seemed to be holding her in an hypnotic trance. Out of the midst of the trance she spoke again, and it was plain to Weldon, as he listened to her low, intent voice, that her thoughts were not upon the sea nor yet upon him.

"It ought to terrify me," she said. "I mean the war, of course. I ought to dread the going out into the atmosphere of it. I don't. Sometimes I think I must have fighting blood in my veins. Instead of being frightened at what my father writes me, I feel stirred by it all, as if I were ready for anything. I went out to Aldershot, one day last year; but that was only so many dainty frills, so much playing soldier. That's not what I mean at all." Turning suddenly, she looked up directly into Weldon's dark gray eyes. "One of my cousins wants to be a nurse. She lives at Piquetberg Road, but she has been visiting friends who live in Natal on the edge of the fighting, where she has seen things as they happen. In her last letter, she told me that she was only waiting for my uncle's permission to go out as a nurse."

"Is that what you would do?"

Her head lifted itself proudly.

"No. She can take care of the wounded men, if she chooses. For my part, I'd rather cheer on the men who are starting for the front. If I could know that one man, one single man, fought the better for having known me, I should feel as if I had done my share."

She spoke with fiery vigor; then her eyes dropped again to the dancing waves. When at length she spoke again, she was once more the level-voiced English girl who sat next him at the table.

"You are going out to Cape Town to stay, Mr. Weldon?" she asked, with an accent so utterly conventional that Weldon almost doubted his own ears.

"To stay until the war ends," he replied, in an accent as conventional as her own.

"In Cape Town?" Then she felt her eyes drawn to meet his eyes, as he answered quietly,--

"I shall do my best to make myself a place in the firing line."

Again her conventionality vanished, and she gave him her hand, as if to seal a compact.

"I hope you will win it and hold it," she responded slowly. "I can wish you nothing better."

CHAPTER TWO

A berugged, bedraggled bundle of apologies, Miss Ophelia Arthur lay prone in her steamer chair, her cheeks pale, her eyes closed. Her conscience, directed towards the interests of her charge, demanded her presence on deck. Once on deck and apparently on guard, Miss Arthur limply subsided into a species of coma. Her charge, meanwhile, rosy and alert, sat in the lee of a friendly ventilating shaft. Beside her, also in the lee of the ventilating shaft, sat Mr. Harvard Weldon.

The past week had been full of the petty events which make up life on shipboard. The trail of smoke from a passing steamer, the first shoal of flying fish, the inevitable dance, the equally inevitable concert and, most inevitable of all, the Sabbatic contest between the captain and the fresh-water clergyman who insists upon reading service: all these are old details, yet ever new. Throughout them all, Weldon had sturdily maintained his place at Ethel's side. By tacit consent, the girl had been transferred to the motherly care of Mrs. Scott who, after a keen inspection of Weldon, had decided that it was safe to take upon trust this clean-eyed, long-legged Canadian who was so obviously well-born and well-bred.

Now and then Carew joined the group; but the handsome, dashing young fellow had no mind to play the part of second violin. He would be concertmaster or nothing. Accordingly, he withdrew to the rival corner where a swarthy little French girl maintained her court without help from any apparent chaperonage whatsoever. Left in possession of the field, Weldon made the most of his chances. The acknowledged attendant of Ethel, his jovial ministrations overflowed to Mrs. Scott, until the sedate colonel's wife admitted to herself that no such pleasant voyage had fallen to her lot since the days when she had started for India on her wedding journey. Weldon had the consummate tact to keep the taint of the filial from his chivalry. His attentions to Mrs. Scott and Ethel differed in degree, but not in kind, and Mrs. Scott adored him accordingly. One by one, the languid days dropped into the past. Neptune had duly escorted them over the Line, to the boredom of the first-class passengers and the strident mirth of the rest of the ship's colony. Winter was already behind them, and the late December days took on more and more of the guise of summer, as the log marked their passing to the southward. To many on board, the idle passage was a winter holiday; but to Weldon and Carew and a dozen more stalwart fellows, those quiet days were the hush before the breaking of the storm. Home, school, the university were behind them; before them lay the crash of war. And afterwards? Glory, or death. Their healthy, boyish optimism could see no third alternative.

For ten long days, Miss Ophelia Arthur lay prone in her berth. Her hymnal and her Imitation lay beside her; but she read less than she pondered, and she invariably pondered with her eyes closed and her mouth ajar. On the eleventh day, however, she gathered herself together and went on deck. With anxious care Weldon tucked the rugs about her elderly frame. Then he exchanged a glance with Ethel and together they sought the shelter of the ventilating shaft.

Nothing shows the temperature more surely than the tint of the gray sea. It was a warm gray, that morning, and the bowl-like sky above was gray from the horizon far towards the blue zenith. From the other end of the ship, they could hear the plaudits that accompanied an impromptu athletic tournament; but the inhabitants of the nearest chairs were reading or dozing, and the deck about them was very still. Only the throbbing of the mighty screw and the hiss of the cleft waves broke the hush.

Out of the hush, Ethel spoke abruptly.

"Do you know, Mr. Weldon, you have never told me what brings you out here."

He had been sitting, chin on his fists, staring out across the gray, foam-flecked water. Now he looked up at her in surprise.

"I thought you knew. The war, of course."

"Yes; but where are you going?"

"To somewhere on the firing line. Beyond that I've not the least idea."

"Where is your regiment now?"

"I haven't any."

She frowned in perplexity.

"I think I don't quite understand."

"I mean I haven't enlisted yet."

"But your commission?" she urged.

"I have no commission, Miss Dent."

"Not--any commission!" she said blankly.

In site of himself, he laughed at her tone.

"Certainly not. I am going as a soldier."

She sat staring at him in thoughtful silence.

"But you are a gentleman," she said slowly at length.

Weldon's mouth twitched at the corners.

"I hope so," he assented.

"Then how can you go as soldier, for I suppose you mean private?"

Dictated by generations-old tradition, the question was eloquent. Weldon's one purpose, however, was to combat that tradition; and he answered calmly,--

"Why not?"

"Because--because it isn't neat," she responded unexpectedly.

This time, Weldon laughed outright. Trained in the wider, more open- air school of Canadian life, he found her insular point of view distinctly comic.

"I have a portable tub somewhere among my luggage," he reassured her.

She shook her head.

"No; that's not what I mean. But you won't be thrown with men of your own class. The private is a distinct race; you'll find him unbearable, when you are really in close quarters with him."

Deliberately Weldon rose and stood looking down at her. His lips were smiling; his eyes were direct and grave. His mother could have told the girl, just then, that some one had touched him on the raw.

"Miss Dent," he asked slowly; "is this the way you cheer on the men?"

She flushed under his rebuke and, for a moment, her blue eyes showed an angry light.

"I beg your pardon. I was referring to the men whom I am likely to know."

"And omitting myself?" he inquired.

"You are the exception which proves the rule," she answered a little shortly. "Of course, I wish you all good; but I don't see how it is to be gained, if you bury yourself in the ranks."

"It may depend a little upon what you mean by good," he returned, with a dignity which, notwithstanding her momentary petulance, won her full respect. "I am not going out in search of the path to a generalship. Fighting isn't my real profession."

"Then what are you going for?" she demanded sharply. With no consciousness of dramatic effect, his eyes turned to the Union Jack fluttering above them.

"Because I couldn't stay away," he answered simply. "From Magersfontein to Nooitdedacht, the pull on me has been growing stronger. I am not needed at home; I can shoot a little and ride a good deal. I am taking out my own horse; I shall draw no pay. I can do no harm; and, somewhere or other, I may do a little good. For the rest, I prefer the ranks. It's not always the broadest man who lives entirely with his own class. For a while, I am willing to meet some one outside. As soon as I get to Cape Town, I shall enlist in a regiment of horse, put on the khaki and learn to wind myself up in my putties. Then it will remain to be seen whether my old friends will accept Trooper Weldon on their list of acquaintances."

"One of them will," the girl said quickly. "If only for the sake of novelty, I shall be glad to know a man in the ranks."

He shook his head.

"No novelty, Miss Dent. I know any number of fellows who are doing the same thing. We can't all be officers; a few of us must take orders. Out in the hunting field, we say it is the thoroughbred dog who answers to call most quickly."

She ignored his last words.

"And you don't even know where you are going?" she asked. "To Cape Town."

"But after that?"

"To my banker. After that, to the nearest recruiting station."

"So you'll not stop in Cape Town?"

Weldon's quick ear caught the little note of regret in her voice.

"Not long. Long enough, however, to pull any latch-string that offers itself to me."

Her eyes dropped to the shining sea.

"My mother will offer ours to you," she said quietly. Then she added, with a swift flash of merriment, "And you will wish to see Miss Arthur again."

Weldon cast a mocking glance over his shoulder at the recumbent, open-mouthed form.

"Is the lady going to stop long with you?" he queried.

"Long enough to recover from her invalidism."

"To judge from her greeny-yellow cast of countenance, that may take some time. But tell me, Miss Dent, does she always sleep out loud like this?"

"Not always. It usually comes when she is taking what she calls forty winks."

"Then may a merciful heaven prevent her from taking eighty," Weldon observed piously. "Still, the sleeping cat--"

"Fox," she corrected him promptly.

"Fox be it, then. Miss Arthur seems to me to be feline, rather than vulpine, though." Bending forward, the girl studied her chaperon thoughtfully.

"She really isn't so bad, Mr. Weldon. She means well. It is only that I don't like tight frizzles and a hymn-book in combination. People should always have one point of absolute worldliness."

"Aren't fizzles--that is what you called the thatch over her eyebrows; isn't it?-- aren't they worldly?"

Ethel Dent laughed with the consciousness of a woman's superior knowledge.

"It depends upon the season," she replied enigmatically, as she rose.

It was five days later that Ethel closed and locked her steamer trunk. Leaving Miss Arthur to grapple alone with the cabin bags, the girl went out on deck. Regardless of the glaring sunshine of New Year morning, groups of people were dotted along the rail, staring up at the flat top and seamy face of cloud-capped Table Mountain. In the very midst of a knot of eager, excited men, Weldon was leaning on the rail, talking so earnestly to Carew that he was quite unconscious of the girl, twenty paces behind him. She hesitated for a moment. Then, as she walked away to the farther end of the deck, she told herself that Weldon was like all other men, regardful of women only when no more vital interest presented itself. Already she regretted the girlish vanity which had dictated the choice of the gown in which she was to go ashore. For all the young Canadian was likely to know to the contrary, she might be clad in a calico wrapper and a blanket shawl, rather than the masterpiece of a London tailor.

The Dunottar Castle was forging steadily ahead through the blue waters of Table Bay. Beyond the bay, Cape Town nestled in its bed of living green, backed by the sinister face of Table Mountain, and fringed with a thicket of funnels and of raking masts. To the girl, familiar with the harbor when Cape Town had been a peaceful seaport, it seemed that the navies of the world were gathered there before her eyes. It seemed to her, too, that the low, squat town never looked half so fair as it did now, viewed from a softening distance and ringed about with its summer setting of verdure.

Already the docks were in sight and, far to her left at the other end of the long curve of the water front, her keen eyes could make out the roof which, six years before, she had learned to call home. She could imagine the stir and excitement in that home: the controlled eagerness of her busy father, the gentle flurry of her invalid mother, and the tempestuous bulletins issued by the small brother whose occasional letters, full of incoherent affection and quaint bits of orthography, had added interest to the last years of her English life. One and all, they were loyally intent upon her coming. And she, ingrate that she was, could spare thought from the dear home circle to waste it upon the forgetful young Canadian who was talking horse and politics by the rail.

She turned sharply, as Weldon's voice fell upon her ears.

"Happy New Year, Miss Dent! It is an odd wish to be giving, with the mercury at ninety."

With her London gown, she had also donned her London manner, and her answer was banal.

"But none the less welcome, for all its being so warm. May I return it?"

He laughed, like the great, overgrown boy that he so often showed himself.

"I decline to take it back. And where have you been, all the morning?"

"Packing my steamer trunk. I have been on deck for nearly an hour, though."

"I'm sorry I missed so much of the time. I don't see why I didn't see you," he said regretfully. "I was over there by the rail with Carew and a lot of the other fellows, watching the town show up. It was mighty interesting, too, this getting one's first glimpse of a new corner of the earth."

Most men would have seemed penitent over their absorption in other things. Weldon merely acknowledged it as a matter of course, and allowed the girl to draw her own conclusions. She drew them accordingly. At first, they antagonized her. Later on, she admitted their justice. Meanwhile, she kept her momentary antagonism quite to herself, as she looked up into the face of her companion, an earnest, manly face, in spite of its boyish outlines.

"It is hard for me to realize that you are a stranger here," she answered him. "All the way out, you have given the impression of having made the voyage any number of times."

"In what way?"

"In the way of getting what you wish in an utterly matter-of-course fashion." Her laugh belied her London exterior and belonged to the broad felt hat and the soft blouse of the past two weeks.

"That is the one compliment I most value, Miss Dent."

"See that you continue to live up to it, Mr. Weldon."

For an instant, they faced each other, a merry boy and girl. Then Weldon's lips straightened resolutely, and he bowed.

"I will do my best," he answered slowly.

Half an hour later, he joined her at the gangway and took forcible possession of her hand luggage.

"Surely," he said, in answer to her objections; "you will let me do you this one last little service."

"Not if you call it that," she said quietly. "Our acquaintance is only just beginning. If you are to be in Cape Town for a day or two, come and let my mother thank you for your kindness to me, all the way out."

He took her hand, outstretched in farewell.

"Even if I come as Trooper Weldon?" he asked with a smile.

And she answered, with a prophecy of whose truth she was as yet in ignorance,--

"Trooper Weldon will always be a welcome guest in our home."

Then her father came to claim her. When she emerged from his welcoming embrace, she saw Weldon, cap in hand, bowing to her from what appeared a most unseemly distance. The next moment, he had vanished in the crowd.

CHAPTER THREE

According to one's individual point of view, Cape Town, on that New Year morning of nineteen hundred and one, was either a point of departure for the front, or a city of refuge for the sleek and portly Uitlanders who thronged the hotels and made too audible mourning for their imperiled possessions. Viewed in either light, it was hot, crowded and unclean. From his caricature of a hansom, Weldon registered his swift impression that he wished to get off to the front as speedily as possible. The hansom contributed to this impression no less than did the city. Out of a multitude of similar vehicles, he had chosen this for its name, painted across its curving front. The Lady of the Snows had obviously been christened as a welcome to the scores of his fellow colonials who had gone that way before; and he and Carew had dashed past Killarney and The Scotch Thistle, to take possession of its padded interior.

It was almost noon, as they drove through the Dock Gates, past the Amsterdam Battery, and turned eastward towards Adderley Street and the Grand Hotel. It was nightfall before their luggage was safe through the custom house and in their room. Carew eyed his boxes askance. Weldon attacked the straps of his nearest trunk.

"Wherefore?" Carew queried languidly from the midst of a haze of smoke.

"To take account of stock."

"What's the use?"

"To find out what we need, of course."

"But we don't need anything. We've tobacco for our pipes and quinine for our stomachs and fuller's earth for our feet. What more can a man need?" As he spoke, Carew hooked his toe around a second chair, drew it towards him and promptly converted it into a foot-rest. "Besides," he added tranquilly; "to-morrow is Boxing Day, and the bank won't be open until the day after. You know you can't buy anything more than a pink-bordered handkerchief out of your present supplies."

Weldon laughed.

"Don't be too sure I can make out even that," he said, as he dived into the trunk and pulled out a Klondyke sleeping-bag.

Carew watched him from between half-closed lids.

"Going beddy?" he inquired.

"Confound it, no! I thought my calling kit was in there." A pair of dark gray blankets landed in the corner on top of the sleeping-bag.

"That looks jolly comfortable. You'd better bunk in there, and leave the bed to me," Carew advised him. "You're in the wrong trunk for your calling clothes, anyway. What under heaven do you want of them, Weldon?"

"I don't want them to lie all in a heap."

"They'll lie in heaps for a good long time, before you are out of this country," Carew predicted cheerfully. "Moreover, from the look of the place, you could make calls in either pajamas or khaki, and it would pass muster. I saw one fellow, this noon, in evening clothes and a collar button. Besides, there isn't anybody for us to call on."

Weldon smiled contentedly, as he drew out a frock-coat and inspected its satin-faced lapels.

"Not for you, perhaps," he observed quietly.

"Oh, I see." Carew puffed vigorously. "So you have a bidding to call upon Miss Dent."

Weldon dislodged Carew's feet from the extra chair and utilized the chairback as a temporary coat-rack.

"No; quite the contrary," he replied. "I am invited to call upon Miss Ophelia Arthur. Now you will please to keep quiet, for I think I shall go to bed."

In silence, Carew watched him half through the process of undressing. Then, emptying his pipe and snapping open its case, he rose and faced his friend.

"Weldon," he said sententiously; "we don't care to hang around this place longer than we must; and we shall have all we can do to get ourselves enlisted and our horses into condition. We haven't time for much else. I hope you will remember that you came out here, not to fuss the girls, but for the fuss with the Boers."

From his seat on the edge of the bed, Weldon eyed him amicably.

"Don't preach, Carew," he answered coolly. "It doesn't do my soul any good, and it only renders you a bore. It has always been a clause of my creed that two good things are better than one."

Nevertheless, in spite of his haste to unpack his calling clothes, it was full three days later that Weldon turned his face eastward in search of the home of Ethel Dent. Moreover, in all those three days, he had given scarcely a thought to the companion of his voyage. Notwithstanding his first impressions, Weldon had found much to interest him in Cape Town. The streets, albeit unlovely, were full of novel sights and the patter of novel tongues. Cape carts and Kaffirs, traction engines and troopers, khaki everywhere and yet more khaki, and, rising grimly behind it all, the naked face of Table Mountain covered with its cloth of clouds! It was all a tumult of busy change, bounded by the unchanging and the eternal. For one entire morning, Weldon loitered about the streets, viewing all things with his straightforward Canadian gaze, jostling and jostled by turns. War had ceased to be a myth, and, of a sudden, was become a grim reality; yet in the face of it all his courage never faltered. His sole misgivings concerned themselves with the contrast between the seasoned regulars marching to their station, and his boyish self, full of eager enthusiasm, but trained only in the hunting field, the polo ground and the gymnasium. Then, gripping his hope in both hands, he resolutely shouldered his way into the nearest recruiting office. He went into the office as Harvard Weldon, amateur athlete and society darling of his own home city. He came out as Trooper Weldon of the First Regiment of Scottish Horse.

He spent the next morning in sorting over his miscellaneous luggage. In the light of Cape Town and the practical advice which had been his for the asking, his outfit appeared comically complete. Two thirds of it must be stored in Cape Town; of the other third, one full half must be left with the negro servants at the hotel. His toilet fixtures would have been adequate for a Paris season; his superfluous rugs would have warmed him during a winter on the apex of the North Pole. It was with something between a smile and a sigh that he stowed away the greater part of his waistcoats and neckties, in company with the silver-mounted medicine chest by which his mother had set such store. It was as Carew had said: quinine and tobacco were the main essentials.

Then, for the last time in many months, he arrayed himself in black cloth and fine linen, chose his stick and gloves with care, and, leaving Adderley Street behind him, turned eastward towards the home of the Dents.

He found Ethel on the broad veranda, bordered with flower-boxes and overlooking the garden and the blue waters of Table Bay. Dressed in a thin white gown which, to Weldon's mind, was curiously out of keeping with all his preconceived notions of January weather, she rose and came forward to greet him at the top of the steps.

"At last," she said cordially, while she gave him her hand. "I began to fear you had already gone to the front."

"Not without seeing you again," he answered, as he followed her back to the bamboo chairs at the shaded western end of the veranda. "In fact, I began to be rather afraid I should never see the front at all."

"What do you mean?" she asked quickly. "Has something happened since I saw you?"

"A great deal has happened. The thing I referred to was my first sight of British regulars."

Her face cleared.

"Oh, is that all?"

"It is a good deal," he assured her, as he sat down. "I came out here with all sorts of high notions regarding volunteers."

"Well?" she questioned smilingly.

"Well, they have been taken out of me. An untrained man isn't worth much in any line, least of all in the firing line. Still, it would be very ignominious to go back home again."

Her eyes swept over his alert, well-groomed figure.

"And when do you start for the front, Trooper Weldon?"

"How do you know I start at all?"

"How do I know you are sitting opposite me?" she asked lightly. "Having eyes, I use them."

"And they tell you--?" he responded.

"That you are looking content with life."

The laughter died out of his eyes.

"I am," he said gravely; "perfectly content. I am enrolled in the Scottish Horse, and I go tomorrow."

"The Scottish Horse?" she asked quickly. "Which squadron?"

"Do you know anything of it?"

"A little," she answered; "but that little is good. Then it is to Maitland that you are going?"

"Are you omniscient, Miss Dent?"

"No; merely an inquisitive girl who remembers the answers to the questions that she asks. My father, you know, is in the thick of things, and it seems to me I have met half the British army, in the four days I have been at home."

"Officers, or Tommies?" he reminded her.

She laughed at the recollection of her former prejudice.

"You told the truth, Mr. Weldon. One of the men I danced with, last season, is riding across Natal in the same squadron with his groom. In my one London season, I met only officers. Out here, I find Lord Thomas turned into Tommy Atkins, and I meet him every day. But, aside from the war, what do you think of Cape Town?"

"What would I think of Table Mountain without its tablecloth?" he parried. "In both cases, the two things seem inseparable."

"Wait till you know the place better, then," she advised him. "It really does have a life of its own, apart from its military setting."

"I am afraid there's not much chance of my knowing it better," he answered a little regretfully.

"Maitland is only three miles away, and you've not met my mother yet," she suggested.

"Is she at home now?" Weldon asked, with the conscious air of a man suddenly recalled to his social duty.

"Not this afternoon. She has taken Miss Arthur for a drive through Rondebosch. That is quite one of the things to do, you know."

"I didn't know. Is the redoubtable Miss Arthur well?"

The dimple beside the girl's firm lips displayed itself suddenly, and her eyes lighted.

"Wonderfully. Her convalescence has been remarkably short. More remarkable still is the fact that she has neglected to mention her illness to any one."

"How soon does she go back?"

The blue eyes met his eyes in frank merriment.

"Not until she has finished informing my mother of the present London code of chaperonage."

Weldon raised his brows.

"Then I shall find her here, when I come back at the end of the war."

She made no pretence of misunderstanding him.

"Are you so much less strict in Canada?"

"We are--different," he confessed. "Miss Arthur's lorgnette would be impossible with us. I don't mean the lorgnette itself; but the acute accent which she contrives to give to it. Mrs. Scott is more of a colonial matron."

"Dear little lady! Have you seen her since she landed?"

"Once. They are at the Mount Nelson, and Carew and I called on them there. They are leaving for De Aar, Monday."

"And what about Mr. Carew?"

"He goes with me to Maitland. He is Trooper Carew now."

The girl sat staring thoughtfully out across the lawn.

"I wonder what sort of a soldier he will make," she said, half to herself. Weldon faced her sharply.

"Why?"

"Because life is an embodied joke to him."

Weldon rose a little stiffly. His call had lasted its allotted time; nevertheless, under other conditions, it might have lasted even longer. He liked Ethel Dent absolutely; yet now and then she had a curious fashion of antagonizing him. The alternations of her cordial moments with her formal ones were no more marked than were the alternations of her viewpoint. As a rule, she looked on life with the impartial eyes of a healthy-minded boy; occasionally, however, she showed herself hidebound by the fetters of tradition, and, worst of all, she wore the fetters as if they lay loosely upon her. At such moments, he longed acutely to impress her with his own point of view, as the only just one possible.

"I think perhaps you don't fully understand Carew, Miss Dent," he said courteously, yet with a slight accent of finality. "He laughs at life like a child; but he lives it like a man. I have known him since we were boys together; I have never known him to shirk or to funk a difficult point. If the Scottish Horse ever sees the firing line, it will hold no better trooper than Harry Carew."

He bowed in farewell and turned away. Looking after him, Ethel Dent told herself that Weldon's simple words had been descriptive, not only of his friend, but of his loyal, honest self.

Half-way across the heart-shaped bit of lawn enclosed within the curve of the drive, Weldon met another guest going towards the steps. There was no need of the trim uniform of khaki serge to assure him that the man was also a soldier. The starred shoulder straps were needless to show him that here was one born to command. Glancing up, Weldon looked into a pair of keen blue eyes exactly on a level with his own, took swift note of the full, broad forehead, of the black lashes contrasting with the yellow hair and of the resolute lines of the shaven chin. Then, mindful of his frock-coat and shining silk hat, he repressed his inclination to salute, and walked steadily on, quite unconscious of the part in his life which the stranger was destined to play, during the coming months.

CHAPTER FOUR

Sitting in the lee of the picket fence which bounded Maitland Camp on the west, Paddy the cook communed with himself, and Weldon and Carew communed with him.

"Oh, it's long and long yet before a good many of these ones will be soldiers," he, observed, with a disrespectful wave of his thumb towards the awkward squad still manoeuvering its way about over the barren stretch of the parade ground. "They ride like tailors squatting on their press-boards, and they salute like a parrot scratching his head with his hind paw. A soldier is like a poet, born, not made."

In leisurely fashion, Weldon stretched himself at full length and drew out a slender pipe.

"Paddy, if you keep on, I'll fire a kopje at you," he threatened.

Paddy disdained the threat.

"Glory be, the kopjes be riveted down on the bottom end of them! But it's the truth I'm telling. Half of these men is afraid of their lives, when they're on a horse."

"The horses of South Africa are divided into two classes," Carew observed sententiously; "the American ones that merely buck, and the cross-eyed Argentine ones that grin at you like a Cheshire cat, after they have done it. Both are bad for the nerves. Still, I'd rather be respectfully bucked, than bucked and then laughed at, after the catastrophe occurs. Paddy, my knife has been splitting open its handle. What's to be done about it?"

"Let's see."

Bending forward, Carew drew the black-handled knife and fork from the coils of his putties. In the orderly surroundings of Maitland Camp, there was no especial need of his adopting the storage methods of the trek; nevertheless, he had taken to the new idea with prompt enthusiasm. Up to that time, it had never occurred to him to bandage his legs with khaki, and then convert the bandages into a species of portable sideboard.

"Paddy," Weldon remonstrated; "don't stop to play with his knife. No matter if it is cracked. So is he, for the matter of that. Go and tell your menial troop to remember to put a little beef in the soup, this noon. I am tired of sipping warm water and onion juice."

"What time is it, then?"

"My watch says eleven; but my stomach declares it is half-past two. Trot along, there's a good Paddy. And don't forget to tie a pink string to my piece of meat, when you give it to the orderly. Else I may not know it's the best one." With a reluctant yawn and a glance upward towards the sun, Paddy scrambled to his feet and brushed himself off with the outspread palms of his stubby hands. Then he turned to the men behind him.

"Stick your fork back in your putties, Mr. Carew, and I'll send you a knife to go with it. As long as Paddy manages the cooking tent, the cracked knives shall go to the dunderheads. The best isn't any too good for them as rides like you and Mr. Weldon, and drinks no rum at all."

Weldon eyed him mockingly.

"And gives their ration of rum to Paddy," he added. "Go along, man, and set your kettles to boiling, while you return thanks that you know a good thing when you see it."

"Paddy is a great boy," Carew observed, as the little Irishman saluted them in farewell, then turned and strolled away in the direction of his quarters.

"And, what's more, a most outrageously good cook," Weldon assented. "If Paddy's ambition to shoot a gun should ever be fulfilled, England might gain a soldier; but it would lose a chef of the cordon bleu."

"If I were to choose, I'd sacrifice his sense of taste for the sake of keeping his sense of humor," Carew returned. "Not even war can subdue Paddy."

With a disdainful gesture, Weldon pointed out across the sun-baked parade ground with the stem of his pipe.

"War! This?" he protested. "It is nothing in this world but a Sunday school picnic."

And Carew, as his eyes followed the pointing pipe-stem, was forced to give his assent.

It was now five days since, with scores of their mates, Weldon and Carew had been passed from their medical examination to the double test of their riding and their shooting. Elated by their threefold recommendation, they had lost no time in donning their khaki and taking up their quarters under the fraction of canvas allotted to them. The days that followed were busy and slid past with a certain monotony, notwithstanding their varied routine. From morning stables at seven until evening stables at six, each hour held its duty, for in that regular, clock-marked life, recreation was counted a duty just as surely as were the daily drills.

Carew, trained on the football field, took to the foot drill as a duck takes to water. Weldon was in his glory on mounted parade. One summer spent on an Alberta ranch had taught him the tricks of the broncho-buster, and five o'clock invariably found him pirouetting across the parade ground on the back of the most vicious mount to be found within the limits of Maitland. More than once there had been a breathless pause while the entire squadron had waited to watch the killing of Trooper Weldon; more than once there had been an utterly profane pause while the officers had waited for Trooper Weldon to bring his bolting steed back into some semblance of alignment. The pause always ended with Weldon upright in his saddle, his face beaming with jovial smiles and his horse ranged up with mathematical precision. The delays were by no means helpful to discipline. Nevertheless, the officers yielded to the inevitable with the better grace, inasmuch as no one else would voluntarily trust life and limb to the vicious beasts in which Weldon's soul delighted.

Twice already, during the past five days, Weldon had handed over to the authorities a chastened and obedient pony, and had made petition to select a fresh and untrammelled spirit. The one of the afternoon before had been the most untrammelled he had as yet attempted. The contest had begun with the first touch of the saddle. It had continued with Weldon's being borne across the camp on the back of a little gray broncho who was making tentative motions towards a complete handspring. By the time the pony was convinced of the proper function of her own hind legs, Weldon found himself being driven from the door of the cooking tent by Paddy and a volley of potatoes. The broncho surveyed Paddy with scorn, rose to her hind legs and strolled towards the corner of the camp sacred to visitors. There she delivered herself of one final, mighty buck. When Weldon regained the perpendicular, he found himself directly facing the merry, admiring eyes of Ethel Dent. By Ethel's side, mounted on a huge khaki-colored horse, sat the man he had met, only the week before, in the driveway of the Dents' home.

Scarlet with his exertions, grimly aware that his sleeve was pulled from its armhole and his left puttie was strained out of its usual compact folds, nevertheless Weldon saluted her smilingly and, his mount well in hand, galloped off in search of his squadron. That night, however, his clear baritone voice was missing from the usual chorus about the camp fire; and, as he thoughtfully drained his tin billy of coffee, next morning, he was revolving in mind the relative merits of his banker and a dead mother-in-law, as excuses for demanding a pass to town, that afternoon.

However, afternoon found him moodily riding about the camp. His body was on a subdued gray broncho; his mind was solely upon Ethel and her companion. He liked the girl for herself, as well as for the fact that, in this remote corner of the world, she represented the sole bit of feminine companionship which is the rightful heritage of every son of Eve. True, there was Miss Arthur; but Miss Arthur was antediluvian. Under these conditions, it was galling to Weldon to see Ethel absorbed by a comrade who, he frankly admitted to himself, was far the more personable man of the two. And the girl's blue eyes had laughed up into the eyes of the stranger just exactly as, two short weeks before, they had laughed up into his own. Then the little gray broncho jumped cornerwise, and Weldon had difficulty in impressing upon her that handsprings were not an approved form of cavalry tactics. Nevertheless, he did it with a word of apology. For the moment, the broncho was not wholly responsible for her return to evil ways.

Over their breakfast, next morning, his five tentmates fell to catechising him as to his pensive mood, and their catechism was largely intermingled with chaff.

"Paddy's compliments, and roll up for your tucker," the mess orderly proclaimed, as he came into the tent, brandishing a coffee pot in one hand, the frying pan in the other.

Fork in hand, Carew nevertheless paused to take exception to the word.

"I confess I can't see why Tucker, when it is supposed to untuck the creases of us," he observed. "Hermit, shall I serve you in the corner; or will you deign to join us about the festive frying pan?"

"What's the matter with Weldon, anyhow?" another of the group queried, as dispassionately as if the subject of discussion had been absent in Rhodesia. "His face is a yard long, and his lips hang down in the slack of the corners."

"Brace up, man, and get over your grouch," a third adjured him. "You are worse than O'Brien was, the morning after he was shoved in kink. Were you in Cape Town, last night?"

"Not a bit of it," Carew put in hastily, while he buried his knife-blade in the nearest pot of jam. "My left ear can prove an alibi for him. From taps till midnight, Weldon discoursed of all the grewsome things in the human calendar."

The smallest of the group turned himself about and peered up into Weldon's face.

"Homesick, man?" he queried.

"Sure," Weldon replied imperturbably.

"Oh. Then get over it. Just dream of the days when the bronchos cease from bucking and the Stringies shoot no more. Meanwhile, if you could look pleasant, as the photographers say, it would help on things wonderfully."

But the mess orderly interrupted. He had tidings to impart, and they burned upon his tongue.

"Have you heard about Eaton-Hill?" he asked, in the first pause that offered itself.

Five faces turned to him with gratifying expectancy. Eaton-Hill had come out on the Dunottar Castle. He was known to them all as the acknowledged exquisite of the entire camp.

"What about him?"

"C. B. I met him coming out of the orderly room."

"Hm! Camp scavenger. Eaton-Hill will like that," Weldon commented dryly. "What's the row about?"

"Cupid apparently. He went calling in Cape Town, last night, without leave, stayed till past eleven and undertook to come in by sea. He shipped in a leaky boat with a crew composed of one Kaffir boy; the Kaffir funked the surf; they had an upset and Eaton-Hill waked up the picket by the fervor of his swearing at the half-drowned Kaffir."

"Poor Eaton-Hill! Both his morals and his clothes must have suffered," Carew suggested. "Weldon, take warning. Next time you go to call on Miss Arthur, start early and be sure you have your pass pinned to the lining of your coat."

"Who is Miss Arthur?" demanded the chorus.

Deliberately Carew helped himself to the last of the bacon. Then he made answer, with equal deliberation,--

"Miss Arthur is Weldon's lawful chaperon."

At four o'clock, that afternoon, Weldon arose reluctantly from his seat on the western end of the Dents' veranda.

"Parade at five, Miss Dent, and Maitland Camp is four miles away."

Without rising, she smiled up into his waiting eyes.

"You made more than four miles an hour, when Captain Frazer and I were watching you, the other day, Mr. Weldon."

"Yes, twenty at least. Still, as you may have noticed, my mount doesn't always choose the straightest course. If she elects to go to Maitland by way of Durban, it will take me all of the hour to make the journey."

She laughed at his words. Then of a sudden her face grew grave.

"They've no right to give you such a horse, Mr. Weldon."

"Right? Oh, I beg pardon. I chose it."

"Is your life so unhappy?" she questioned, in mocking rebuke.

"It is no suicidal mania, Miss Dent," he reassured her. "I like the rush and excitement of it all; but I had a summer on a ranch, and I learned the trick of sitting tight until the beast tires itself out. Broncho-busting is only a concrete form of philosophy, after all."

"And must you really go?" she asked him.

He lingered and hesitated. Then, with a glance at the horse fastened to a post in the drive below, he straightened his shoulders.

"I must."

She rose to her feet.

"Good afternoon, then."

"And good by," he added.

"What does that mean?"

"That we leave Maitland Camp in the morning."

"I am sorry," she said, and her voice showed her regret. "Where are you going?"

"To Maitland station. Then into a train. Beyond that, I do not know."

"I am sorry," she repeated; "but very glad. It is time you were doing something. I know you didn't take all this journey out here for the sake of being drilled in Maitland Camp until the end of time. We shall miss you; but you will come back to us, some day, and tell us all the story of your deeds. Success to you, Trooper Weldon!"

She gave him her hand; then stood looking after him, as he went down the steps. Once in the saddle, he turned back to wave a farewell to the tall girl framed in the arching greenery that sheltered the broad veranda. Then, urging on his horse, he went galloping away, his boyish face turned resolutely towards the front.

Careless of the oldtime superstition, the girl watched him out of sight. Then slowly she moved back to their deserted corner where she sat long, her elbows on the arms of her chair and her chin resting on her hands. Her eyes were held steadily on Table Bay; but her thoughts followed along the road to Maitland Camp--and beyond.

CHAPTER FIVE

That January had brought the second irruption of Boers into Cape Colony. In reality, they were near Calvinia; but, by the middle of the month, rumor had so far out-stripped fact that certain refugee Uitlanders were ready to affirm that Table Mountain was held by an invading army who patrolled the summit, coffee pot in one hand and Bible in the other. Under these conditions, the little Dutch church at Piquetberg Road had become, in all truth, the abiding-place of the Church Militant.

In deference to tradition, the altar had been promptly pulled down and its ornaments stowed away to be safe from possible desecration. The altar rail was left, however, and Weldon sat leaning against it, his eyes vaguely turned upwards to the organ in the farther end of the church. From the open floor between, the buzz of many voices and the smoke of many pipes rose to the roof; from the vestry room behind him, he heard the cleaner-cut accent of the officers. Outside, above the light spatter of rain on the windows, he could hear the horses stamping contentedly in the leafy avenue without the churchyard wall, and the brawl of the stream beyond. The twilight lay heavy over the church, heaviest of all over the distant organ gallery, where Weldon could barely make out a single figure moving towards the bench. There was a rattle of stops, a tentative chord or two and then a few notes of this or that melody, as if the player, albeit a musician, found himself continually thwarted by the darkness and the absence of any printed notes.

"Who is up there, Weldon?" Carew asked, as he peered up into the dimness.

"Shut up; can't you?" Weldon ordered him abruptly.

And Carew subsided, just as the unseen organist, apparently abandoning his more ambitious efforts, with sure touch swept into the familiar harmonies of the Eventide Hymn, and then, still with his hymnal in mind, jerked out the dozen stops and set the air rocking to the steady beat of Onward, Christian Soldiers.

As he listened, Weldon's mind went backward to his last Sunday evening in the cathedral at home. He had known why the old rector had chosen that time-worn hymn for a recessional; he could still feel the stir of the congregation as he passed them, still see the scarlet blot of color made by his own hymnal against his stiffly starched cotta, still see his mother, erect and pale, staring at him with a resolute bravery which matched his own. Since then, he had been inside no church until to-day. It was a far cry from worshipping in the Gothic cathedral to camping in the simple little Dutch church; but in each the air was vibrating to the same martial hymn.

Little by little, the groups scattered over the floor fell into silence. Here and there, one took up the refrain, now humming it softly, now singing it with full voice. Then the refrain died away; there was an instant's hush, an instant's modulation; and, as a man, the crowd beneath rose to their feet and stood, pipe in hand, while slowly, steadily from the organ came rolling down the familiar notes of God Save the Queen.

The organ was closed with a muffled clatter, the organist rose and slowly came down to the floor. With a friendly word here and there, he passed among the troopers who saluted him and then settled themselves again for comfort and their pipes. Last of all, he paused beside Weldon.

"It is good to put my fingers on the keys again," he said, as he sat down for a moment on the low rail. "We had an organ at home, and I miss it. I builded better than I knew, when I chose this place for our barracks. One rarely finds an organ out here."

Just then an orderly lighted the chancel where they stood. The organist gave a slight exclamation of surprise.

"Isn't this Trooper Weldon?"

The speaker's face was in shadow. Only the starred shoulder straps gave Weldon any clue to the rank of his companion.

"It is," he answered briefly.

"Miss Dent has spoken of you. In fact, we were together at Maitland Camp, last week, when you tried issues with the little gray broncho."

As he spoke, he moved slightly, and the light fell full upon his yellow hair and on his blue eyes, dark and fringed with long black lashes. Weldon looked up at him with a smile of recognition.

"It is Captain Frazer, then?"

"Yes. I am congratulating you on having won your way into Miss Dent's good graces. She tells me you were most thoughtful for her, all the way out."

"You have known Miss Dent for a long time?" Weldon queried.

Captain Frazer answered the question as frankly as it was asked. For the moment, they were man and man. In a moment more, they could resume their formal relations of captain and soldier.

"I knew her well in England. We met at one or two house parties, a year ago last fall. I was at her coming-out function, too." Then he rose. "I shall see you again," he added formally. "Now I wish to make my round of the guards." And, turning, he went striding away towards his own quarters in the vestry.

Weldon looked after him thoughtfully. Then he uttered terse judgment.

"Carew, that's a man," he said.

"Quite likely," Carew assented. "Women don't usually wear khaki. Shall we go in search of Paddy?"

They found him smoking tranquilly by the churchyard gate. The old stone wall towering above his head made good shelter from the drizzle; and Paddy, his day's labor done, was leaning back at his ease, exchanging adverse compliments with the half-dozen sentries who patrolled the wall. He hailed Weldon with cordiality.

"Come along here, little Canuck," he called. "There's room for the two of us and fine smoking. Mr. Carew can stay out in the rain. It's worth his while, even then, for the sake of watching that pigeon- toed cockney in the oilskins, him as is stubbing his toes in the sand, this blessed minute."

"Shut up, Paddy," his victim retorted hotly.

"It's you that should shut up and teach the toes of you to walk hushlike. If you go on like this, you living watchman's rattle, the Boers can hear you, clear up in the Transvaal. Tell me, little one, have you seen your captain yet?"

"Captain Frazer?"

"Yes, Captain Leo Frazer, sure as you're a trooper of C. Squadron. You're in luck, boy. There's not a better soldier nor a finer Christian, this side the line. Neptune must have give him an extry scrubbing, when he come over, for he's white he is, all white. Boys!" Paddy spoke in a portentous whisper.

"Let her go," Weldon advised him calmly.

"It goes without letting. Once let Paddy get free of his skillets, once let him have a rifle in place of his spoon, and you'll see war. The Kingdom of Heaven is a spot of everlasting peace. All I ask of Saint Peter is a place in front of a line of Boers and Captain Frazer beside me to give the orders."

"Here he is, Paddy." The low-pitched voice was full of mirth. "He orders you inside your tent to plan up an extra good breakfast. Some of these fellows must volunteer for a night guard out in the open, and they will need a feast, when they come in."

Weldon rose hastily.

"At your service, Captain," he said, just as Paddy, in nowise daunted by the unexpected presence of his superior, responded,--

"Sure, Captain, I put a condition on the tail of it. If you'll remember back a little, you'll see that I merely said, 'when I get a rifle instead of a spoon.' It's a sorry day for an able-bodied man to be tied to a frying pan all his days. Now and then he longs to leap out and get into the fire."

Meanwhile, half of the men inside the church were volunteering for the party of twenty guards demanded by the Captain. It was a surly night, cold and raw with a drizzling rain. Nevertheless, this was their first approach to anything even remotely resembling active service, and the men sought it eagerly.

By dint of attaching himself to the Captain's elbow and assuming that his going was an understood thing, Weldon accomplished his aim. Eleven o'clock found him, wet to his skin, sneaking on the points of his toes through the thick grass beyond the river, with nineteen other men sneaking at his heels. There had been no especial pretext of Boers in the neighborhood; tactical thoroughness merely demanded a guard on the farther side of the river. Nevertheless, the enthusiastic fellows threw themselves into the game with the same spirit with which, twenty years before, they had faced the danger of a runaway by the tandem of rampant hall chairs. A stray Boer or two would have made an interesting diversion; but, even without the Boers, a night guard in the open possessed its own interest.

By four in the morning, the interest had waned perceptibly. The establishment of their force in a convenient hut and the placing of pickets had served to occupy an hour or so. After that, nothing happened. The storm was increasing. The rain beat ceaselessly on the corrugated iron roof of their shelter and made a dreary bass accompaniment to the strident tenor of the rising wind. Inside the but the men yawned and whispered together by turns. Carew's best jokes began to fall a little flat, and Weldon held his watch to his ear, to assure himself that it was still in active service. Then hastily he thrust the watch into his pocket, gathered up his sleeping-bag and removed himself to a remote corner of the hut, with Carew and a dozen more after him.

Not even the most enthusiastic champion of South African rights can affirm that the South African citizen is heedful of the condition of his lesser buildings. The rising wind had proved too much for the hut. Its joints writhed a little, seesawed up and down a little, then yawned like a weary old man. From a dozen points above, the rain came pattering down, seeking with unerring instinct that precise spot on each man's back where skin and collar meet.

"Whither?" Carew queried, as Weldon made his fifth move.

"Outside, to see what the pickets are about."

"But it rains," Carew protested lazily.

"So I observe. Still, I'd rather take it outside as it comes, instead of having a gutter empty itself on me, when I am supposed to be under cover."

"Better stay in," Carew advised him.

"No use. Sleep is out of the question, and I'd rather be moving; it is less monotonous."

"Go along, then, and look out for Boers. Can I have your bag?"

"You're too wet; you'd soak up all the inside of it. If I am to get a chill, I'd rather do it from my dampness than your own." Carew laid hands on the bag.

"What a selfish beast you are, Weldon!" he observed tranquilly. "This is no sack-race; you can't go out to walk in your bag. In fact, it takes two to make a navigable pair. Then why not let me have it?"

"Why didn't you bring your own?"

Already Carew was arranging himself in his new covering.

"I mislaid mine in Cape Town," he replied sleepily. "Now please go away. I need my beauty nap."

An hour later, he was roused by a sharp reversal of his normal position. When he became fully awake, he was lying in a pool of water in the middle of the hut, and Weldon was in possession of the blankets and bag.

"What's the row?" he asked thickly. "I'm a Canadian, out here shooting Boers. Oh, I say!" And he was on his feet, saluting the man at Weldon's side.

"The only bag in the squadron, Captain Frazer," Weldon was explaining. "The blankets are quite dry. Roll yourself up, and you will be warm in a few minutes."

Carew surveyed the transfer with merry, impartial eyes.

"Well, I like that," he said, when the Captain's yellow head was all that was visible above the encircling cocoon. "I thought you said that you preferred to catch cold from your own wetness, Weldon. I was merely damp; this man is a sponge."

Before Weldon could answer, the yellow head turned, and the blue eyes looked up into Carew's eyes laughingly.

"Merely one of the privileges of rank, Carew," the Captain observed as dryly as if he had not risen from his warm bed to swim the river and walk a mile in the darkness and the downpour, in order to see how the new boys were getting on.

CHAPTER SIX

Captain Leo Frazer, age thirty and an Englishman, had a trick of looking Fate between the eyes with those black-fringed blue eyes of his, of accepting its gifts with gratitude, its occasional knocks with cheery optimism. At Rugby he had ultimately been captain of the school; at Oxford he had been of equal prowess in rowing and football. Since taking his degree, he had been a successful doctor in the intervals of time allowed him by his membership in one of the crack regiments at home. He had never seriously contemplated the possibility of active service; but Colenso had been too strong a pull upon him. Leaving some scores of sorrowing patients to bemoan him as already dead, he had promptly shipped for Cape Town. The year of grace nineteen hundred had found him on the scene at most of its exciting events. Where Fate refused to take him, he asserted his strong hand and took Fate, until that weary lady was forced to go hopping about the map of South Africa with the agility of a sand flea.

In battle, Frazer was always in the thickest spatter of bullets, where he bowed himself to the inevitable and lay prone, though with his face turned to one side to give free passage to the chaff which carried his comrades through so many grim hours. In the presence of danger, his humor never failed him. In those sorrowful hours which followed the cessation of firing, no man was in greater demand than he. Many a brave fellow had died with his hand shut fast over Frazer's long, slim fingers; many a man's first, awful moments in hospital had been soothed by the touch of those same firm, slim hands. And in the singsongs around the camp fire, or at the mess table, Frazer's voice was always heard, no matter how great the tumult of a moment before.

Like many another of his countrymen, Captain Frazer had learned lessons since he had left the ship at Cape Town, just a year before. He had come out from England, trained to the inflexibly formal tactics of the British army. Again and again he had seen those tactics proved of no avail in the face of an invisible enemy and an almost inexpugnable country. He had learned the nerve-racking tension of being exposed to a storm of bullets that came apparently from nowhere to cut down the British lines as the hail cuts down the standing grain; he had learned the shock of seeing the level veldt, over which he was marching, burst into a line of fire at his very feet from a spot where it seemed that scarce a dozen men could lie in hiding, to say nothing of a dozen scores. He had learned that, under such fire, a man's first duty was to drop flat on his face, to push up a tiny breastwork of earth and to fire from behind that slender shelter. England could not afford to send her sons over seas for the sake of having them slaughtered by needless obedience to the laws of martial good form. Fighting a nation of hunters, they too must adopt the methods of the hunt. And, most of all, Captain Frazer had learned the imperative need of mounted riflemen. Two months before, while lying up at Durban until his wrist had healed from a Mauser bullet, he had come into close contact with the Marquis of Tullibardine.

As a result of that contact, January had found Captain Frazer in Cape Town, ready to take command of the newly enlisted Scottish Horse.

Now, as he looked over his force at Piquetberg Road, he was congratulating himself that his men were fit for service, very fit. Frazer knew something of men. Experience had assured him that these men were worth training and his months of service under the great Field Marshal had taught him that an officer could be a man among his men, yet lose not one jot of his dignity. Accordingly, Frazer set himself to the task in band. By the time he had been at Piquetberg Road for two days, he knew the name and face of every man in his squadron. A week later he could tell to a nicety which of his men were engaged to girls at home, which of them had heard of one Rudyard Kipling, and which of them could be counted upon in an emergency. The two latter counts Weldon filled absolutely. In regard to the first, Frazer permitted himself a moment of acute uneasiness. It had been in a spirit of unmitigated joy that Frazer had met Ethel Dent in Cape Town, on the morning of New Year's day. In London he had known the girl just well enough to admire her intensely, not well enough, however, to have found out that she had any permanent connection with South Africa. His joy had lasted until the hour of his calling upon her, three days later; then it had received a sudden check. Ethel had been as cordial as ever; nevertheless, her talk had been full of the young Canadian whom he had met in the drive. Frazer was intensely human. After a year of separation he would have preferred to bound the talk by the experiences of their two selves.

As a natural consequence, he had developed a strong prejudice against Weldon; but Weldon, all unconsciously, had done much to remove that prejudice. Not every man could manage a crazy, bucking broncho in any such fashion as that; fewer still could come out of the scrimmage, unhurt, to bow to a young woman with a cordiality quite untinged with boyish bravado. That day at Maitland, Frazer had registered his mental approval of the long-legged, lean Canadian with his keen gray eyes and his wrists of bronze. He had registered a second note of approval, that first night at Piquetberg Road, when Weldon, with no unnecessary words, had contrived to impress upon the mind of his captain that he was to be included in the guard to cross the river. Totally obedient and respectful, Weldon nevertheless had given the impression of a man who intended to win his own way. Moreover, the direction of that way appeared to be straight towards the front.

Meanwhile, peacefully unconscious of this diagnosis, Weldon was sitting on the river bank, prosaically occupied in scooping out the remaining taste left in an almost-empty jam tin. Beside him, Carew was similarly occupied. Two more jam tins were between them and, exactly opposite the pair of jam tins, there squatted a burly Kaffir, young, alert and crowned with a thatch of hair which by rights should have sprouted from the back of a sable pig. His mouth was slightly open, and now and then his tongue licked out, like the tongue of an eager dog. Aside from his hair, his costume consisted of one black sock worn in lieu of muffler and a worn pair of khaki trousers.

Behind him, the river caught the sunset light and turned it to a sheet of flowing copper; beyond stretched the open country in long, waving lines that ended in the deep yellow band of the afterglow. Above them, the sky was blue; but it dropped from the blue zenith to the yellow horizon through every imaginable shade of emerald and topaz until all other shades lost themselves in one vivid blaze of burnt orange. It had been a day of intense heat. Already, however, the falling twilight and the inevitable eastward shift of the wind had brought the first hint of the evening chill.

Weldon shrugged his shoulders.

"Hurry up, Carew," he adjured his companion. "I am for leaving our feast and hieing us back to the sanctuary."

"Right, oh!" Carew raised his jam tin and took careful aim at a rock in mid stream.

Instantly the Kaffir hitched forward.

"Mine?" he demanded.

Carew stayed his arm.

"What for?"

"Eat. Um good."

"Nothing in there but atmosphere, sonny. You can get that out of any box. Suppose I can hit that little black point, Weldon?"

"Not if I know it," Weldon said coolly, as he tossed his own tin to the boy and, seizing that of Carew, threw it after its mate. "Let the little coon have his lick, Carew. It's not pretty to watch him go at it, tongue first; but we can't all be Chesterfields. What is your name, sonny?"

The boy paused with suspended tongue, while he rolled the great whites of his eyes up at the questioner. Then, the whites still turned upon Weldon, he took one more hasty lick.

"Kruger Roberts," he said then, detaching himself for an instant from his treasure. "Oh, I infer you like to sit on fences?" Weldon said interrogatively.

"Ya, Boss."

"Which side do you intend to come down?"

"Me no come down," the boy answered nonchalantly, more from inherent indifference than from any comprehension of Weldon's allegory.

"All right. Stop where you are. Meanwhile, I think I should call you Jamboree."

"Ya, Boss." The face vanished from sight behind the tilted tin. Then it reappeared, and a huge finger pointed to the remaining tins. "Mine, too?"

But already the boy was forgotten. Weldon was following hard on the heels of the sentry who had dashed through the gate in the churchyard wall.

Four o'clock the next morning, that darkest hour which, by its very darkness, heralds the coming dawn, found C. Squadron moving out from the gray-walled churchyard, their faces set towards the eastern mountains. All night long they had stood under arms, ready for the attack which might be at hand. By dawn, they were well on their way towards the laager, fifteen miles distant, whence had come the scouting hand of Boers who, for two days past, had made leisurely efforts to pick off their scattered sentinels. At the head of the little troop rode Frazer. Behind him and as close to his heels as military law allowed, came Weldon, mounted on the same little black horse which had so often carried him to the hunt at home. Horse and rider both sniffed the chilly dawn with eager anticipation. Each knew that something was in store for them; each contrived to impress upon the other his determination to make a record, whatever happened. For one short minute, Weldon let his strong hand rest on the satiny neck. He could feel the answering pressure of the muscles beneath the shining skin. That was enough. He and The Nig were in perfect understanding, one with another.

"Weldon?"

He spurred forward to the Captain's side and saluted.

"In the flurry, last night, I forgot to tell you that Miss Dent comes to Piquetberg Road, to-day. She is to visit a cousin, Miss Mellen; and she wished me to tell you that she hoped you could find time to call upon her."

The Captain spoke low, his eyes, after the first moment, steadily fixed upon the line of hills before them. Weldon answered in the same low tone.

"You have heard from Miss Dent?"

"Yes. A note came, last night. She is to be here for a month, while her uncle is in England on a business trip. Mr. Mellen is the mayor. You probably know the house."

"I can easily find it. Please tell Miss Dent I shall be sure to call as--"

A blinding flash ran along the line of hills close in the foreground where, an instant before, had been only empty ground. There was a sharp crackle, a strident hum and then the muffled plop of bullets burying themselves in the earth six hundred feet in the rear. The Nig grew taut in every muscle; then she edged slowly towards the huge khaki-colored horse that bore the Captain, and, for an instant, the two muzzles touched.

"Too long a range, man. Try it again," Frazer observed coolly, as his glance swept the empty landscape, then, turning, swept the faces of his men.

That last sight was to his liking. He nodded to himself and straightened in his saddle, while the orders dropped from his lips, swift, clean-cut and brooking no question nor delay. Ten men went galloping off far to the southward, to vanish among the foothills and reappear on the pass behind the enemy, while a dozen Boers, springing up from the bowels of the earth, followed hard on their heels. Ten more took the horses and fell back out of range of the firing; and the remainder of the squadron stayed in their places and helped to play out the game.

It was all quite simple, all a matter of course. Instead of the fuss and fume and chaos of fighting, it had worked itself out like a problem in mathematics, and Weldon, as he lay on the ground with his Lee-Enfield cuddled into the curve of his shoulder, felt himself reducing it to a pair of simultaneous equations: if X Britons equal Y Boers on the firing line, and Y Britons draw off the fire of W Boers, then how many Britons--But there came a second flash and a second spatter, nearer, this time; and he lost his mathematics in a sudden rush of bad temper which made him long to fly at the invisible foe and beat him about the head with his clubbed rifle. It was no especial satisfaction for a man in his position to climb up on his elbow and help to discharge a volley at an empty landscape. The war pictures he had been prone to study in his boyhood had been full of twisty-necked prancing horses and bright-coated swaggering men, all on their feet, and very hot and earnest. Here the picture was made up of a row of brown-clothed forms lying flat on their stomachs and, far before them, a single flat-topped hill and a few heaps of scattered black rocks. And this was modern war.

There came a third blaze, a third hum of Mauser bullets. Then he heard a swift intake of the breath, followed by Carew's voice, the drawling, languid voice which Weldon had learned to associate with moments of deep excitement.

"Say, Weldon, some beggar has hit me in the shoulder!"

Then of a sudden Weldon realized that at last he knew what it meant to be under fire.

CHAPTER SEVEN

"Oh, truce! Truce!" Alice Mellen protested. "Don't talk shop, Cooee."

"It's not shop; it is topics of the day," Ethel responded tranquilly. "Besides, I want to hear about Mr. Carew. Is he dangerous?"

Weldon laughed.

"No, for his wound; yes, for his temper. One was only a scratch; the other way, he was horribly cut up."

"Did he swear?" Alice queried, while she distributed lumps of sugar among the cups.

"Alice!"

"Don't pretend to be shocked, Cooee. Even if you haven't been out but one season, you ought to know what happens when a man turns testy. Frankly, I think it is a healthy sign, if a man stops to swear when he is hit. It shows there are no morbid secretions."

"You prefer superficial outbreaks, Miss Mellen?" Frazer inquired, as he handed Ethel her cup.

"Yes. They are far less likely to produce mortification later on," she answered, laughing up into his steady eyes. "What do you do, when you are hit, Captain Frazer?"

"They call me Lucky Frazer, you know," he replied. "I've been in no end of scrimmages, and I was never hit but once."

Bending over, Ethel turned back the cloth and thumped on the under side of the table.

"Unberufen and Absit omen," she said hastily. "Don't tempt Providence too far, Captain Frazer. At my coming-out reception, I met a man who boasted that he always broke everything within range, from hearts to china. Ten minutes later, he tripped over a rug and fell down on top of the plate of salad he was bringing me. And he didn't break a thing--"

"Except his own record," Weldon supplemented unexpectedly. "I suspect he also broke the third commandment. The keeping of that and the falling down in public are totally incompatible."

"And that reminds me, you were going to tell what Mr. Carew did when he was hit," Ethel reminded him.

"I never tell tales, Miss Dent."

"But, really, how does it feel to be under fire?" she persisted.

"Ask Captain Frazer. He has had more experience than I."

She barely turned her eyes towards Frazer's face.

"He is talking to my cousin and won't hear. Were you frightened?"

"No."

"Truly? But you wouldn't confess, if you were."

He blushed at the mockery in her tone.

"Yes. Why not? I expected to be desperately afraid; but I was only desperately angry."

"At what?"

"Nothing. That's the point. There was nothing in sight to be angry at. Bullets came from nowhere in a pelting shower. Most of them didn't hit anything; there was no cloud from which the shower could come. One resented it, without knowing exactly why. It was being the big fellow who can't hit back when the little one torments him."

"Cooee!"

The remonstrance was long-drawn and forceful. This time, Ethel heeded.

"What is it, Alice?"

"Do you remember that, this noon, we agreed not to mention the war? These men fight almost without ceasing. When they aren't fighting, they do sentry and stables and things. This is an afternoon off for them. We really must talk accordingly."

"What are you and Captain Frazer talking about?"

"Cricket and seven-year locusts."

Ethel held out her empty cup.

"Very well. Then Mr. Weldon and I will discuss mosquitoes and seven- day Baptists. No sugar, please, and I'd like another of those snappy things."

"Does that mean a Mauser?" Weldon asked, as he brought back her cup.

"No. I mean biscuits, not cats. But you sinned then. However, my cousin has her eye upon us, so we must be distinctly frivolous. Is there any especially peaceful subject you would like to discuss?"

"Yes. Please explain your name."

She looked up at him with sudden literalness.

"It is for my grandmother. For four hundred years there has been an Ethel Dent in every generation."

"I meant the other."

"Oh, Cooee?" She laughed. "It dates from our first coming out here, when we were children. My old Kaffir nurse--I was only five, that first trip--used to call me so, and every one took it up. We went back to England, after a few weeks, and the name was dropped; but my uncle stayed out here, and he and my cousin always kept the old word."

Weldon stirred his tea thoughtfully.

"I rather like it, do you know?" he said.

"Surely, you don't think it fits me?"

His eyes moved from her shining hair to the hem of her elaborate white gown. Then he smiled and shook his head.

"Not to-day, perhaps. But the Miss Dent of the Dunottar Castle--"

She interrupted him a little abruptly.

"Does that mean I am two-sided?"

"No; only complex."

She smiled in gracious response.

"You did that very well, Mr. Weldon," she said, with a slight accent of superiority which galled him. Then, before he could reply, she changed the subject, speaking with a lowered voice. "And what of the Captain?"

It suited his mood not to understand her.

"In what way?"

"Every way. What do you think of him?"

Then she drew back, abashed by the fervor of the answer, as he said slowly,--

"That the Creator made him, and then broke the pattern."

The little pause which followed caught the alert attention of the hostess, and convinced her that it was time to shift the groups to another combination. A swift gesture summoned Weldon to the table, while Frazer dropped into his vacant chair. Ethel met the Captain with only a half-concealed eagerness. This was not the first time that a consciously trivial word of hers had been crushed out of life by Weldon's serious dignity. She was never quite able to understand his mood upon such occasions. The man was no prig. At times, he was as merry as a boy. At other times, he showed an inflexible seriousness which left her with the vague feeling of being somehow or other in the wrong. The result was a mood of pique, rather than of antagonism. Up to that time, Ethel Dent had known only unreserved approval. Weldon's occasional gravity, to her mind, suggested certain reservations. By way of overcoming these reservations, she focussed her whole attention upon Captain Leo Frazer. Across the table, Weldon, in the intervals of his talk with his hostess, could hear the low murmur of their absorbed conversation.

It had been at Ethel's suggestion that the tea-table had been set, that hot afternoon, under the trees in the heart of the garden. Just at the crossing of two broad walks, a vine-roofed kiosk gave shelter from the late sunshine, while its bamboo screens were half raised to show the long perspective of garden walk and distant lawn. Save for the orange grove at the left and the ash-colored leaves of the silver wattle above them, Weldon could almost have fancied himself in England. The lawn with its conventional tennis court was essentially English; English, too, the tray with its fixtures. There, however, the resemblance stopped. The ebony handmaiden who brought out the tray was never found in private life outside the limits of South Africa. When she sought foreign countries, it was merely as a denizen of a midway plaisance.

"Yes, and their names are their most distinctive feature," Alice assented to Weldon's comment.

"More than their mouths?" he asked, with a flippant recollection of Kruger Roberts engrossed in his jam tin.

"At least as much so," she responded, laughing. "You notice that I called our maid Syb. She told me, when she came, that her old master named her Sybarite. I understood it, the next day, when I found her snoring on the drawing-room sofa."

During the time of her answer, Weldon took his opportunity to look steadily at his young hostess. Up to the moment of the shifting of the groups, he had been too fully absorbed in the pleasure of once more meeting Ethel to pay much heed to any one else. Now he turned his gray eyes upon Alice Mellen, partly from real interest in her personality; partly to counterbalance the rapt attention which Ethel was bestowing upon the Captain. She had been the selfsame Ethel, a bundle of contradictions that attracted him at one moment and antagonized him at the next. He liked her absolutely; his very liking for her increased the sense of antagonism when, for the instant, she departed from his ideals of what she ought to be. And yet, Weldon was candid enough to admit to himself that she departed from them, rather than fell below them. Often as she had antagonized him, she had never really disappointed him.

As for Alice Mellen, he confessed himself surprised. Gathering together all that Ethel had ever told him of her cousin, of her living her entire life out there in the southern end of South Africa, of her desire to be a nurse, he had pieced together an effigy of the combined traits of a Hottentot and a vivandiere. This girl answered to neither description. Her clothes and her manners and her accent all had come, albeit with slow indirectness, from London. Not only would she and her gowns pass muster in a crowd; but furthermore she would end by being the focal point of a good share of that crowd. Nevertheless, Weldon found it impossible to discover her most distinctive point. Even while he sought it, he wondered to himself whether this might not be another cousin of whom he had never heard. The women doctors and nurses at home wore stout shoes and had pockets let in at the seams of their frocks, useful, doubtless, but with an unlovely tendency to yawn and show their contents. This girl was a mere fluff of pale yellow organdie which brought out the purplish lights in her ink-black hair.

"Did you have the heart to disturb her?" he asked, reverting to the subject of Syb's nap.

"I was forced to. She was on all the cushions, and I needed one for myself. She took it in good part, though. She told me she had been disturbed, the night before, by the snoring of the parrot, two rooms away. As a result, she left me feeling that the apology really ought to come from me."

"Is that the way of the race?" Weldon queried, as he set down his empty cup. "If so, you make me tremble."

"Why?"

"Because, without in the least intending it, I have accumulated a boy."

She looked up suddenly.

"How do you mean?"

"I don't know how. It apparently did itself. It was the day before we went out to be fired at, and he said his name was Kruger Roberts, and I fed him some empty jam tins."

"A huge black boy with bristly hair?" she interpolated.

"Yes, and a mouth so large that one wonders how his face can hold it all."

She sat up alertly, resting her folded arms on the edge of the table.

"This becomes interesting. Kruger Roberts is Syb's avowed and lawful lover."

Weldon laughed.

"Mine also, as it appears. As I say, I fed him jam tins. There were four of them, and they were very jammy. Then we became interested in the Boers, and I forgot Kruger Roberts. When I came back, yesterday morning, dead tired and my horse all in a mess, I found Kruger Roberts calmly sitting on my extra blankets, cleaning my shoes with Paddy's best dishcloth. Paddy was in a wild state of mutiny, and told me that that chattering baboon had vowed he was Trooper Weldon's boy. Since then, I have tried in vain to dislodge him; but it is no use. The Nig is like a piece of satin, and it is all I can do to keep my compressed-paper buttons from winking defiance at the Boers on the northern edge of Sahara."

Alice Mellen laughed with the air of one who understood the situation.

"You builded better than you knew, Mr. Weldon, and your jam tins will be no house of cards. The Kaffirs are an unaccountable race of beings, lazy and good-natured. Once let them love or hate, though, and all their strength goes into the working out of the feeling. Kruger Roberts obviously has a sweet tooth; the day may come when your enemies may find it changed to a poisoned fang. Do you want the advice of one who knows the country?"

"I do," he assented heartily.

"Then keep your Kruger Roberts," she said decisively.

"But what shall I do with him?"

"Let him do for you."

"As a valet? I've never been used to such luxury," he protested, laughing.

She shook her head.

"Not only valet. He will be groom, cook, guide, interpreter and, whether you wish it or not, your chum. Moreover, he will do it all with the face of a clown and the manner of a tricksy monkey. As a panacea for the blues, you will find him invaluable."

There was a little pause. Then she added, with a complete change of tone, "My cousin has spoken of you so often, Mr. Weldon."

"And of you," he returned.

The directness of her answer pleased him.

"Then we ought to start as friends, and not waste time over mere acquaintance."

"I thought there were no acquaintances out here," he answered lightly. "In camp, our first question is: Friend, or foe?"

"In the towns, we have every grade between. Often the same person slides through all the grades in a single day. But you haven't answered me."

His eyes met her eyes frankly.

"About the friendship? I thought that wasn't necessary."

"Customary, however," she suggested, with a smile.

"But, as I say, there are no customs here," he retorted. "At least, I should have said so, this morning. Now I am not so sure." Then he laughed. "I've bungled that horribly, Miss Mellen. What I meant was that you have given me a very good time, this afternoon."

"Prove it by coming again," she advised him.

"If I may. I don't wish to wear out my welcome; but one hasn't so many friends in South Africa."

"What about Kruger Roberts?" she reminded him.

"That gives me two."

"And Captain Frazer?"

Weldon's eyes lighted.

"Some day, perhaps. I would be willing to wait for that."

Gravely her glance roved from the alert young Canadian at her side to the older, more steadfast face across the table. Then she shook her head.

"You will not have to wait long, Mr. Weldon?" she said quietly. "Captain Frazer spoke of you, a week ago. I have known him for months; I know what, with him, stands for enthusiasm."

"I wish you might be a true prophet. I would honor you, even here in your own garden. For the sake of Captain Frazer's regard, I would give up most things," he replied, too low to be overheard by the couple who were now chaffing each other above their cooling cups.

Later on, he wondered a little how far the apparent inconsequence of her next question was the result of chance.

"What about Cooee?" she asked, in a voice as low as his own had been.

He hesitated. Then he looked up at her steadily.

"Miss Mellen, I am sure I don't know," he answered gravely.

CHAPTER EIGHT

"Beastly shame that the Boers hadn't buried themselves instead of the guns!" Carew remarked, as he wrestled with a tough thong of bully beef which yielded to his jaws much as an India-rubber eraser might have done.

Without making any pretence of extracting nutriment from his own ration, Weldon converted it into a missile and hurled it straight at his companion.

"There's this difference," he returned pithily; "a gun is a good enough fellow to deserve Christian burial. Carew, do you ever yearn for the fleshpots?"

Without bringing his jaws to a halt, Carew shook his head.

"Do you?" he asked, after a prolonged interval.

"Yes, if they could be brought here; not otherwise. I like the game; but I also like a little more oats mixed with my fodder. How long is it since we had a square meal?"

"How long since we halted in that pineapple grove, coming up from Durban?" Carew retorted. "That made up for a good deal. You have no cause to rebel, though. Between Paddy and Kruger Bobs, you stand in for all the tidbits that are going."

With a mock sigh, Weldon pointed backward over his shoulder.

"But unfortunately Kruger Bobs and The Nig are left behind in the shadow of Naauwpoort's dreary heights. By the way, Carew, does it ever strike you that these Boers make a lot more fuss over their spelling than they do over their pronunciation? At home, we'd get as good results out of dozens less letters."

"They make as good use of their extra letters as they do of their extra bullets," Carew returned tranquilly. "They've been sniping, all the morning long, and they have only hit a man and a quarter now."

"Which was the quarter?"

Turning, Carew displayed a jagged hole in his left sleeve. Weldon laughed unfeelingly.

"Can't you keep out of range, you old target? If there's a bullet coming your way, it's bound to graze you."

"This is only the fourth. Only one of those really meant business. Oh, hang it! There they go again!" he burst out, as a distant line of rocks crackled explosively and, a moment later, a random bullet opened up the side of his shoe.

With the swift change of occupation to which the past four months had accustomed them, they were soon in the saddle and galloping off across the rolling veldt. Before them, a pair of guns were pounding away at the rocky line and its flanking bushes, and beyond, over the crest of the next ridge, scores of thick-set, burly figures were racing in search of shelter, with a fragment of the Scottish Horse in hot pursuit.

Neck and neck in the vanguard raced Weldon and Carew, with Captain Frazer's huge khaki-colored horse hard on their heels. To Weldon, the next hour was one of fierce excitement and pleasure. The shriek of the shells, long since left behind, the flying figures before them, the rise and fall of his own gray little broncho as she stretched herself to measure the interminable veldt, the khaki-colored desert, dotted with huge black rocks and shimmering with the heat waves which rose above it towards the midday sun: his pulses tingled and his head throbbed with the glorious rush of it all.

And then the slouching figures were met by other slouching figures, and reluctantly Weldon drew in his horse, as the halt was ordered. Only madness would prolong the chase against such heavy odds. Mere sanity demanded that the troopers should delay until the column came up. The action must wait, while the heliograph flashed its call for help. Weldon grumbled low into Carew's ear, as the minutes dragged themselves along, broken only by indeterminate volleys.

"I have exactly five rounds left," he said at length. "I believe in obedience, Carew; but, when I get this used up, by jingo, I'll pitch into those fellows on my own account."

"Keep cool," Carew advised him temperately. "You always were a thriftless fellow; you must have been wasting your fire. Oh, I say, what's the row in the rear?"

"The column, most likely. It's time, too. Those fellows would be on us in a minute. Ah ha!" And Weldon drew a quick breath of admiration, as the guns came up at the gallop under the watchful eye of the Imperial Yeomanry.

Once in position on a rise to the left, quickly the guns unlimbered and opened fire, while the sergeants gathered around the boxes of spare cartridges on the ground beside the panting ammunition horse. Then at last came the order for the advance, the order so eagerly awaited by Weldon, maddened by his long exposure to the bullets of his unseen foe. In extended order, the squadrons galloped forward until their goal was a scant five hundred yards away, when of a sudden a murderous fire broke out from the rocks in front of them, emptying many a saddle and dropping many a horse. Under such conditions, safety lay only in an unswerving charge.

Close on their leaders' heels, the troopers spurred forward and, revolver in right hand, rifle in left, they charged over the remaining bit of ground and into the midst of the Boer position. Briton and Boer met, face to face. Revolvers cracked; Boers dropped.

Mausers crashed; Britons fell. And then, through and over, the British charge had passed.

Even then Weldon found no place for pause. From behind the Boer position, a band of their reinforcements came galloping down upon him. Caught between the two lines, the squadrons wheeled about, fell again upon the broken enemy, dashed through them and, amid the leaden hail, retired upon their own guns. And now once more the gunners could reopen fire, and the shells dropped thick and fast. The moment for a general advance had come. In open order, a thousand men dashed forward and reached the ridge, only to see the retiring foe galloping away in all directions across the open veldt. A halt was ordered, to rest the winded mounts. Pickets were thrown out on front and flank, while the British awaited their approaching convoy. That night, the column rested upon the veldt at Vlaakfontein.

After the rush of the day, its hope and its succeeding disappointment, Weldon was long in falling asleep. Carew was out on picket; Captain Frazer, coat off and sleeves rolled to his shoulders, was busy among the wounded, and Weldon had cared to make few other close friends in the squadron. Around him, he could hear the murmurs of other sleepless ones; but he lay silent, his arms under his head, his face turned upward to the shining perspective of the stars. In similar perspective there ranged them-selves before his mind the events of the past twelve weeks.

Already the month at Piquetberg Road seemed a chapter out of another volume. It had culminated in that languid afternoon spent around the tea-table under the wattle tree in the garden, culminated there and also ended there. With the unexpectedness that marks all things in a time of war, the next noon found him steaming across the Cape Flats, with Maitland in sight. Two days later, they were loaded on an empty hospital ship returning to Durban. Piquetberg Road was child's play now, for the front was almost in sight. The voyage had been beastly; but after it had come the real beginning of things. Natal, in those days of late February, had seemed deserving of its name, a true Garden of Africa. The crossing was now a memory of heavy grades, of verdant country, of ripened fruits. There had been the week's delay at Pietermaritzburg where they had tasted a bit of civilization in the intervals of completing their outfits; there had been the brief stop at Ladysmith, already recovered from her hardships of the year before, then the crossing the border into the Transvaal where the verdure slowly vanished to give place to the dreary wastes of red- brown veldt. At Johannesburg, he had manufactured an excuse for a long letter to Ethel who- -

"Show a leg there!"

The sergeant's voice at his ear called him back to the realities of life. He sat up as alertly as if he had slept upon eider-down.

By eight o'clock, Weldon was out on the veldt, two miles from camp. Before him, a force of Yeomanry was guarding the two guns; around him, a detail from his own squadron protected the flank on the right. And, still farther to the right, a cloud of yellowish smoke rose skyward across the yellower sunshine. Then, of a sudden, out from the heart of the wall of smoke came a muffled thud and roar, confused at first, growing strident and more detached until, sweeping from the haze of smoke, five score Boer horsemen rode in a bolt-like rush, fierce and uncheckable. Without swerving to right or left, they charged straight towards the Yeomanry drawn up beside the guns, drove them back and shot down the gunners almost to a man. An instant later, the guns were whirled about and trained upon their quondam owners.

From over his breakfast, that morning, the General raised his head to listen to the booming of the fifteen-pounders. No need to tell him that heavy fighting had begun. His experienced ear had taught him that magazine firing meant business. His hand went in search of his field-glasses.

"General, the enemy have captured the guns. The Major asks for assistance to retake them."

The General lowered his glasses. Covered with dust, and breathless, Weldon was before him.

"Mount every available man, and gallop to the scene of action!"

Orderlies carried the command to the different regiments. Before the mounted men could start, the infantry were half-way to the guns. But already shells were falling into the camp, telling every man that the guns were in the hands of the Boers.

In the forefront of the remainder of his squadron, Weldon found himself borne onward in the rush, straight from the camp to the right flank of the guns. The broncho's swinging trot had long since changed to a gallop, and her eyes were flashing with the wicked light of her old, unbroken days, as she went tearing across the sun- baked veldt, up and down over the rises and through the rare bits of thicket at a pace which Weldon would have been powerless to check. He had no mind to check it. The crisp air, full of ozone and warmed by the sun, set his cheeks to tingling with its impact. A true rider, he let his mood follow the temper of his horse and, like a pair of wild things, they went bolting away far towards the head of the squadrons.

And always the firing of the guns grew nearer and faster and more murderous.

He took no note of passing moments, none of the miles he had ridden during the past days. These counted for naught, while, with photographic distinctness, the picture before him fixed itself sharply in his mind: the dust-colored troops on the dusty veldt, the brown-painted guns, the distant line of the enemy's fire and, far to the eastward, the wall of smoke which was fast sweeping towards them from the acres of burning veldt.

"Captain Frazer, the General orders you to take up your position in the kraal on the extreme right, and to hold it at any cost."

From his place at the Captain's side, Weldon glanced at the orderly, then, turning, looked across the veldt to the four gray walls surrounding the clump of trees a mile away. His hand tightened on the curb, and he straightened in the saddle, as the Captain led the way into the purgatory beyond, an orderly purgatory, but crossed with leaden lines of shot and shell.

At such moments, the brain ceases to act coherently. When Weldon came to himself, he was kneeling behind the old gray wall, revolver in hand, firing full in the faces of the Boer horsemen, scarce fifteen feet away. Carew, his right foot dangling, had been hustled to the rear of the kraal where the gray broncho and her mates were in comparative shelter.

"Weldon?"

He looked up in a half-dazed fashion. The wall of smoke was already shutting down about the retreating Boers. Beside him stood the Captain, his yellow hair clinging to his dripping face, his blue eyes, under their fringe of black lashes, glittering like polished gems. Coated as he was with dust and sweat, his clothing torn and spotted with the fray, he looked ten times more the gallant gentleman, even, than when he had met Weldon in the heart-shaped bit of lawn encircled by the Dents' driveway. Now he held out his hand.

"Splendidly done, old man! One doesn't forget such things."

CHAPTER NINE

Captain Frazer had scarcely finished speaking, when the voice of the General sounded in their ears.

"A plucky attack and a plucky defeat, Captain Frazer. Kemp is a man worth fighting. You are not wounded?"

"Thanks to Trooper Weldon," the Captain told him, with a smile.

The General's keen glance included them both.

"Good! And now can you spare me a trusty man? One who can ride? I must have some despatches at Krugersdorp before midnight. I should like some one from your squadron."

The eyes of Captain Frazer and Weldon met. Again the General's keen glance was on them both; then it concentrated itself upon the younger man.

"I am ready," he answered to its unspoken question.

"You are sure you are fit? It is forty miles, and the rain will be on us inside of an hour."

"It makes no difference."

As he spoke, Weldon felt himself surveyed from hat to shoelace.

"Very well. Get yourself fed, and come to my tent in an hour. It will be better to wait until dusk before starting, for these hills are infested with Boers. Do you know the country?"

"Partly. I can learn the rest."

"You need a remount."

Weldon stroked the little gray broncho.

"If I had my own horse. Otherwise, I prefer this. I can trust her, even if she is tired."

Again the glance swept him over, beginning at the boyish face, resolute and eager beneath its streaks of red-brown dust. Then, as Weldon saluted, the General turned and rode away, with the Captain at his side.

"You've the making of a man there, Captain Frazer," was his sole comment.

Weldon, meanwhile, was allowing the little gray broncho to pick her own dainty way out of the shambles about her feet. Then, once free from the litter of men and horses, he turned her head to the spot where, he had been told, his squadron were gathering together their diminished forces. As he rode slowly onward, he was surprised to see how low the sun had dropped. The fighting must have lasted longer than he had thought. It had been hot and heavy; but at least he had not funked it. For so much he could be thankful. In so far as he could recall any of his emotions as he had dashed into range of the pitiless firing, they had been summed up in a dull rage against the enemy, mingled with a vague hope that no harm should come to the plucky little mount. Just one instant's pause he could remember. That was when he had put forth all his strength to check her pace until he could readjust a strap that was plainly galling her. And afterwards? Not even the thoroughbred Nig could have played her part in the fight with more steady gallantry. Stooping, he eased the bit and patted the firm gray neck where the mane swept upward for its arching fall.

"Boss?"

He straightened in his saddle.

"Kruger Bobs! By all special providences, where did you come from?"

"Naauwpoort. Kruger Bobs come bring Nig to Boss."

"Kruger Bobs, you're a genius."

Kruger Bobs vanished behind his smile.

"Ya, Boss," he replied then. "Boss all right?"

"Yes, all right."

"Dutchmans no killed Boss?"

"No."

Doubtfully Kruger Bobs shook his sable bristles. He had heard the firing, such firing as he had never dreamed of until then, and it seemed to him impossible that any man could come unscathed out of the heart of it. Of Weldon's being in the very heart of it, no doubt had once stained the loyal whiteness of his soul. To assure himself of Weldon's safety, he ambled around the gray broncho in a clumsy circle. The gray broncho showed her appreciation of the attention by nipping viciously at the flank of his horse. By Weldon's left side, Kruger Bobs halted and pointed an accusing forefinger at his knee.

"Dutchmans hurt Boss," he said anxiously.

"Where?"

"Dere." In spite of his effort for sternness, the voice of Kruger Bobs quavered with anxiety.

Bending over, Weldon glanced down at the dark red stain on the coil of khaki serge. Then, all at once, he remembered the sudden stinging of his leg, just before he had started the gray broncho on her last mad rush across the lead-swept plain. In the excitement that followed, the matter had entirely passed out of his mind. Even now that his attention was called to it, he was conscious of no physical discomfort.

"Kruger Bobs go for doctor?" the boy was urging.

Weldon laughed reassuringly.

"It's nothing, Kruger Bobs. I've no time to fool with doctors now."

"What Boss do?"

"Feed Piggie, eat something, look up Mr. Carew and then get to the General's tent, inside an hour."

"What for de big boss soldier?"

"He wants me."

"Ya?" Kruger Bobs demanded uneasily.

"To ride a despatch."

"Despatch!" Kruger Bobs exploded in hot wrath. "Kruger Bobs go despatch; Boss go bed." "Can't do it, Kruger Bobs. This is war, and I've given my word to the General. It was an order, and I had to do it." Backing his horse off for a step or two, Kruger Bobs sat looking at his master and shaking his head mournfully. Then he straightened in the saddle.

"Boss go; Kruger Bobs go, too," he said, with steady decision.

Less than an hour later, outside the General's tent Kruger Bobs sat astride The Nig, with the rein of the gray broncho in his hand. The clouds, since noon banked low in the eastern horizon, had swept up across the sky, and already the rain was pattering drearily over the hunched-up shoulders of Kruger Bobs. Inside the tent, the colloquy was brief. Twice Weldon repeated over the substance of his despatches and his instructions regarding their destination. The despatches were slipped between the layers of his shoe-sole, the cut stitches were replaced, and Weldon rose to his feet.

"My nigger has come from Naauwpoort, bringing me a fresh mount," he said then. "May I take him with me?"

"What is he?"

"A Kaffir."

"From where?"

"Piquetberg Road."

"Can you trust him?"

Weldon's eyes met the eyes of the General steadily. "As I would trust myself," he answered.

Five minutes later, Weldon passed out of the tent door. At his quarters, he dismounted and went in search of a blanket. Muffled in the thick folds, the horses' feet would make no sound on the hard-baked earth. Kruger Bobs, meanwhile, went out to reconnoitre in order to discover a possible gap in the line of Boer pickets.

The pickets once passed, Weldon mounted once more and, with Kruger Bobs following close behind, rode carefully away into the inky, drizzling night. For the first hour, he rode steadily and with comparative comfort. The excitement of the battle was still in his blood, its noises ringing in his head, its sights dancing like will- o'-the-wisps before his eyes. Later, the inevitable reaction would follow, and the inevitable weariness. Now, refreshed by their supper, both he and the broncho had come to their second wind, and they faced the storm pluckily and with unbowed heads. Beside him, The Nig, fresh and fit as a horse could be, galloped onward steadily under the weight of Kruger Bobs. It had been at Weldon's own command that Kruger Bobs had abandoned his raw-boned steed and placed himself astride the sacred body of the thoroughbred Nig. On such a night and after such a battle, a horse abandoned was a horse forever lost. Neither The Nig nor Piggie could be left to any chance ownership, but neither could Piggie, fresh from a two-day fight, be left to the mercies of an inexperienced rider. Three inches shorter than his master, Kruger Bobs weighed fifty pounds the more, and he rode with the resilient lightness of a feather bed.

Weldon's hour of rest had been divided in strict ratio between himself, his friend and his horse. For fully half that period, he and Kruger Bobs had rubbed the sturdy gray legs and anointed the scratched neck with supplies taken from the portable veterinary hospital always to be found in the recesses of the Kaffirs scanty garments. Then, snatching a hasty meal, with the last of it still in his hands, Weldon strode away to look for Carew. He found him, bandaged but jovial, a shattered bone in his foot and his pipe in his shut teeth. Fortunately the pain bore no relation to the seriousness of the case, and Weldon left him to his pipe, cheered by the doctor's assurance that two or three weeks would bring him back into fighting trim. Carew's own disrespectful comments on the injured foot were still in his ears, as he entered the tent of the General.

By degrees, the night grew dark and darker. Riding eastward with their backs to the southerly storm, nevertheless now and again the wind swirled about fiercely, to send the lashing rain against their faces. Under their feet, the dusty veldt turned to mire, from mire to a pasty glue, and from glue to the consistency of cream. Bottom there was none; the bottomlessness of it only became more apparent when one or other of the horses stumbled into the hole of an ant- bear. Twice the gray broncho was on her knees; once The Nig came down so sharply that Kruger Bobs rolled forward out of his saddle, to land on his back, nose to nose with his astonished mount. Worst of all, the fever of the fight was dying out from Weldon's veins. His pulses were slowing down, and the ceaseless jar of the gray broncho's gallop waked his wounded leg to a pain which fast became intolerable.

Kruger Bobs edged closer to his side.

"Boss sick?" he asked.

"Not altogether content, Kruger Bobs."

"Leg?" the boy questioned anxiously.

"Yes; that--and some other things."

"Me help Boss?"

"No, thank you. I'd better let the mess alone."

"Boss ride Nig?" Kruger Bobs suggested, in the hushed tone in which all their talk had been carried on.

"It is better not to change."

The silence broadened, broken only by the splashing of eight hoofs in the ever-deepening mire, and by the sighing squeak of wet strap rubbing on wet strap. Then Kruger Bobs spoke again.

"Paddy send," he said, as he poked a soft parcel into Weldon's dangling hand. "He say 'Give it to little Canuck.'"

Weldon felt and tasted his way into the parcel. It was large, and filled with savory bits which Paddy must have gleaned here and there from the general mess, robbing freely from many a greater man, all for the sake of the "little Canuck."

It was no time for the discipline which bids a servant eat of the crumbs from his master's table. For the hour, Kruger Bobs and he were friends, bound upon one and the same errand. With impartial hand, Weldon tore the paper across and divided its contents. He only regretted that convention had forbidden him the trick of smacking his lips in sign of relish. It would have been good to have the ability of Kruger Bobs to give audible token of his appreciation of Paddy's bounty.

Somewhat refreshed, he straightened in his saddle.

"Now be careful, Kruger Bobs. There are Boers in these hills," he warned his companion; "and it would never do for us to be sniped."

Kruger Bobs came close to his side.

"Dutchmans kill Kruger Bobs, no matter; kill Boss, no take despatch. Boss say to Kruger Bobs where de despatch. Kruger Bobs take him to Krugersdorp, if Boss die."

And Weldon shivered a little, as the silence dropped again.

The ridges were steeper now, and came in more swift succession, as the horsemen plodded wearily along the southern slope of the Rand. Piggie was breathing heavily; and Weldon, clinging to his saddle with the purely mechanical grip of the exhausted rider, halted again and again to rest the plucky little animal whose best was always his for the asking. Of his own condition he took no heed. It was all in the game. He would play the game out as long as he could; but his last move should be, as his first had been, strictly according to rule. Meanwhile, for two facts he was at a loss to account. Dawning was still hours distant. Nevertheless, the darkness before him was blotted and blurred with alternating waves of blue and gray. The veldt was empty; yet, above the roar of the rain around him, an odd purring sound was in his ears. Then everything lost itself in his determination not to allow the saddle to slip from between his tired knees.

He roused himself at the challenging voice of a picket.

"Despatches for General Kekewich," he answered, in a voice which seemed to his own ears to have come from miles away.

"Advance and give the countersign."

Irritably he gathered himself together.

"I can't, I tell you. I don't know your blasted countersign. I've despatches from Dixon to General Kekewich. Take me to him at once."

The colloquy lasted for moments, in a drawn battle of determination. Its stimulus had waked Weldon from his lethargy; it had also waked again that fierce and throbbing pain below his knee. He left the sentry in no doubt, either of the truth of his statement, or of his mood. Then, with Kruger Bobs at his side, he plodded forward towards the lights of the town, while he braced himself for a final effort.

Fifteen minutes later, he reached the second line of pickets. The gray broncho's head drooped pitifully, as Weldon sat waiting for the inevitable challenge. It came at last; and Weldon's answering voice was slow with a weakness which was not all feigned.

"Despatches from Dixon's column. Take me to the Commandant, please."

He was dimly aware of a hand on his bridle, dimly conscious that Piggie was being led forward for a seemingly endless distance. As they halted in front of a gray stone building, Weldon dimly heard the tingling of many bells within, then the hurried opening of a window, and a voice demanding the cause of the disturbance below. He felt himself going fast; but, gripping his will with all his might, he pulled himself together long enough to answer,--

"Despatches for General Kekewich between the soles of my left boot."

Then he pitched forward on his broncho's neck.

CHAPTER TEN

"Twelve inches make one foot, six feet make one man, sixty men make one troop, four troops make one squadron," the monotonous voice ran on. Then it came to an unexpected finale. "And three squadrons make the Boer army run."

The man in the next bed giggled. His wound was in his shoulder, and it had left his sense of humor unimpaired. As a rule, the fighting records of the wounded never came inside that long, bed-bordered room; but there were few within it now who were ignorant of the plucky ride made by the lean, boyish-looking Canadian trooper. A part of the story had come by way of the doctor in charge of the ambulance train which had brought him from Krugersdorp to Johannesburg, a part of it had come from the trooper's own lips, and that was the most tragic part of it all.

Below, in the courtyard of the hospital, Kruger Bobs squatted on his heels in the sun and waited. Now and then, he vanished to look after the creature comforts of The Nig and the little gray broncho; now and then he shuffled forward to demand news from some passer-by whose sleeve was banded with the Red-Cross badge. Then he shuffled back to his former post and sat himself down on his heels once more. Kruger Bobs possessed the racial traits which make it an easy matter to sit and wait for news. He was also an optimist. Nevertheless, his face now was overcast and rarely did it vanish behind the spreading limits of his smile.

For four days, Weldon lay prostrate and babbled of all things, past, present and to come. Three names dotted his babblings. One was that of his mother, one of his captain, and the third that of Ethel Dent. With all three of them, he appeared to be upon the best of terms. Finally, on the fifth day, he suddenly waked to the fact that a woman was bending above him, to wipe his face with a damp sponge.

He was too weak to rise. Nevertheless, he straightened himself into a rigid line, and addressed her with dignity.

"I beg your pardon. Please don't wash my face for me," he said, in grave displeasure.

She smiled down at him, with the air of a mother smiling at a fretful child. The smile irritated him.

"Doesn't it refresh you?" she asked quietly.

"No," he answered, with flat, ungracious, mendacity.

"I am sorry. You have been sleeping heavily, and--"

He felt his mind slipping out of his own grasp, and he strove to hold it in his keeping.

"No matter now," he interrupted hastily. "Please get me--"

She waited in silence. Then she asked encouragingly,--

"What shall I get you?"

The mind was almost gone; but still he held fast to the edge of it, as he murmured,--

"Some bully beef."

The nurse turned away. Her lips were smiling; but her eyes clouded, as the babbling began once more.

Twenty-four hours later, she was greeted by a white-faced, clear- headed trooper.

"Good-morning, nurse," he said coolly. "You see I am better."

"Much better, Mr. Weldon," she assented cordially. He looked puzzled. "I thought we fellows in hospital had no names, nothing but numbers," he answered.

"It depends. When one meets an old friend, the number isn't quite the right name for him."

Turning slightly, he stared up at her with the impassive curiosity of a man just coming back from The Unknown. Then he shook his head.

"I am afraid--" he began slowly.

With a quick gesture, she took off her crisp white cap, uncovering a heavy pile of ink-black hair. "There!" she said, with a smile. "Does that make me look more natural, Mr. Weldon? I am Alice Mellen, Cooee Dent's cousin."

Instantly he put out his hand, sunburned still, but curiously thin. The smile on his lips was the boyish, frank smile which Alice had seen and liked, that afternoon in the garden at home.

"What good angel brings you here?" he asked eagerly.

"No angel; merely the lady who rules over the household of Mars. I am glad to find you again, even if the Johannesburg hospital isn't a good place for a man. But you mustn't talk now. Later, we can make up for lost time."

Impetuously his fingers shut on a fold of her apron. Then his native instincts and his years of training asserted themselves, and he let go once more. Nevertheless, his eyes were appealing.

"Don't go."

"But I must," she answered, her hands busy with her cap.

Her tone showed that, like himself, she too had learned the meaning of an order. He yielded to its quiet firmness.

"If you must. But, before you go, tell me this: have I been off my head?"

She nodded in assent.

He frowned.

"Sorry," he said briefly. "Please answer me honestly. Have I mumbled things and made a blasted fool of myself?"

It was still two days before he was allowed to talk to his own satisfaction. Then, one afternoon in her rest hour, Alice Mellen let him have his way and, seated by his cot, she answered tersely to a raking fire of terse questions.

"How long have I been here?"

"Just a week."

"How did I get here?"

"Hospital train from Krugersdorp."

"What for?"

"You had a touch of fever. We could treat you better here." Her replies were man-like in their brevity.

"Fever? I thought it was a Mauser bullet."

"It was. Your leg was not so bad; but the long ride and the exposure to the storm--"

He interrupted her.

"What do you know about my ride?" he asked.

Her answer showed that the woman was not lost in the nurse.

"Everybody knows of your ride. Even in these days of plucky deeds, we are proud of you."

He shook his head, though the color came into his cheeks, brown beneath their pallor.

"It was nothing. I did my duty."

"So Kruger Bobs has informed us."

"Kruger Bobs? Is he here?"

This time, she laughed outright.

"I should say he was. For a week, he has been sitting exactly in the path of the doctors, waiting for news. Twice he has been ordered off; but he merely hitches over to the other end of the steps and refuses to budge farther. We discovered him, the first night you were here, by having the bead surgeon fall headlong over him, as he went down the steps. Kruger Bobs doesn't show up well, on a dark night."

Weldon clasped his hands at the back of his head.

"If I thought you were using American slang, Miss Mellen, I should contradict you," he answered, with a touch of his old humor. "I can remember at least one dark night when Kruger Bobs made an excellent showing."

She nodded.

"We have bad a few Americans here before, Mr. Weldon. I think I understand."

"How long have you been here?" he asked, after a pause.

"Ten weeks."

"And you like it?"

"Why else should I be here?"

"From a sense of duty."

"Is that what brought you out?"

"No. My coming was inevitable. It seemed a part of me that I couldn't help."

"But you wished to come?" she queried.

"Of course. But that was only a Dart of it. I have wished to do things before, and have done them. This was quite different. It all seemed a part of Fate, and I walked through it, like a puppet with somebody else's hand pulling the strings." He paused and shook his head. "It is no use. I can't make you understand it. I acted freely and did just what I chose; but yet, all the time, I felt as if it had all been arranged for me, whole generations ago."

Thoughtfully she bent forward, straightened the coverings above his wounded leg; then sat up again. Then she shook her head a little regretfully.

"No," she said. "I am afraid I don't understand. Perhaps it is because I am selfish; but I usually feel as if I made my plans, regardless of Fate."

"What about our meeting here?" he asked quizzically.

She answered in the same tone.

"Wait until we see what comes out of it. Fate, if one believes in such a thing, only works in an endless chain."

"And the broken links?"

"According to your notion, there should be none," she retorted. "Fate ought to be a better workman than that."

"Than what?"

"Than spoiling her work as she goes along. If there's any chain at all, it should be endless and durable. But a man with a Mauser hole in his leg and a fever in his head has no business to be talking of Fate. Let's talk about Ethel, instead."

He settled himself back comfortably.

"Perhaps it amounts to the same thing, in the long run."

"Perhaps. I don't see how, though. Anyway, Ethel wouldn't be pleased with the notion. She is absolutely independent, and generally arranges things according to her own sweet will."

"Where is she now?"

"In Cape Town," Alice answered, quite unaware of her own lack of truth.

"And well?"

"Gloriously. In fact, as far as I can learn, Cooee always is well. Just now she is having a wonderfully gay time. Since Lord Roberts went back to England, Cape Town has been full of people, resting there before sailing for home."

"Resting?"

"Haven't they earned the right?" she questioned, in swift challenge to the quiet scorn in his tone.

"Even if the battles are over, the fighting isn't," he answered tersely. "The glory doesn't lie entirely in the pulverizing the Boer army; there's a little left for the men who are sweeping up the pieces."

Her trained eye saw the rising color in his face. Swiftly she changed the subject.

"Glory for all, enough and to spare," she replied. "But, as I say, Cape Town is crowded with officers, lying up for repairs, and Ethel is queen bee among them. It's not only for herself; it is what you would call Fate. She happens to be the only girl of her set who is just out from London; she had met a good many of them there, and now she is holding a veritable salon. She even has one sacred teacup, set up on a high shelf ever since the day that Baden-Powell used it."

Weldon smiled.

"Miss Dent is a hero-worshipper," he commented.

"So are we all, in certain directions. Moreover, most women like their heroes to have a little personality. One can't make one's admiration stick to a blank wall of impersonal perfection."

Weldon's mind moved swiftly backwards to two blue, black-fringed eyes glowing out from a dust-streaked face.

"No," he assented; "but neither can one ever really be chums with his hero. Or, even if he can, he doesn't care to try the experiment."

Alice glanced at her watch, rose, then lingered.

"I am not so sure of that," she replied thoughtfully. "I want the pedestal of my hero to be a low one; and Cooee declares that she wishes no pedestal at all. If her hero is worthy of the name, he must bear inspection even from above. The worst flaw of all might lurk in the very crown of his head."

Half an hour later, she came back again.

"Mr. Weldon, do you feel strong enough to see Kruger Bobs for exactly five minutes?" she asked.

The gray eyes lighted.

"For ten times five," he answered eagerly.

Kruger Bobs shuffled in upon the heels of an orderly. Under his bristly hair, his face was a study of mingled emotions which culminated in his mouth. A grin of pure happiness had drawn up the upper lip; at sight of his prostrate master, the lower one was rolling outward in a sudden wave of pure pity. Beside the cot, he halted and stood looking down at Weldon with eyes which, for the moment, transformed his lazy, jolly, simian face into a species of nobility. Lying back on his pillow, Weldon waited for him to speak, waited with an odd, restless beating of the heart for which he was wholly at a loss to account.

The pause between them lengthened. At last Kruger Bobs drew his mangy brown felt hat across his eyes.

"I's here, Boss," he said simply.

However, it was enough.

The next morning found Weldon sitting up. A clean-cut hole through the flesh of a man who has lived a clean-cut life is swift in healing. Now that his fever had left him, his superb vitality was asserting itself once more, and he rallied quickly. Meanwhile, it was good to be able to sit up and eat his breakfast like a civilized being. Weldon had all the detestation of the average healthy being for invalid ways. Moreover, he longed to be up and doing. With his growing strength, the orderly, noiseless routine of the hospital came upon his nerves. One of the nurses always walked on the points of her toes; and he was conscious of a wild longing to throw a pillow at her, as she went diddling to and fro past him, a dozen times a day. The doctor, a man of iron nerve and velvet hand, was a daily delight to him. And there was always Alice, frank, friendly and altogether enjoyable. During the past three days, their liking had grown apace. Absolutely feminine, yet with the healthy impersonality of a growing boy, Alice Mellen was a born comrade, and Weldon enjoyed her just as, in her place, he would have enjoyed Carew.

She came down the ward, that morning, and paused beside his chair.

"You look like your old self at last," she said, as she held out her hand in congratulation.

"I might echo your words," he answered, while he looked up into her eyes, shining with merriment and with something that yet seemed to him closely akin to annoyance. "Granted the apron, you might be pouring tea at home."

"Not tea; but malted milk, in these latter days," she said, laughing. "But I am about to retire from your case. May I introduce your new nurse, Mr. Weldon?"

His reluctant assent was changed to eager greeting. Light, swift steps came down the room; a tall figure stopped at his side in the full glare of a sunshiny window which all at once seemed focussing its light upon waving strands and heaped-up coils of vivid yellow hair.

"Cooee!" Then, too late, he bethought himself of his manners and tried to bite the word off short.

Linking her arm in that of her cousin, the girl stood looking down at him with merry, mocking blue eyes.

"Invalids are supposed to have privileges denied to well men," she answered demurely. "It might perhaps be Cooee here, to-day; but it will have to be Miss Dent, to-morrow, when you are back in the field again. After all, it is hardly worth while to make the change, Trooper Weldon."

CHAPTER ELEVEN

Upon one side, at least, the meeting between the two cousins on the previous night had been wholly unexpected.

Late that afternoon, an ambulance train had come in, loaded with men from the over-crowded field hospital at Krugersdorp, and for hours Alice had been in ceaseless attendance upon the surgeon in charge. Little by little, the girl had found her nerves steadying down to the task in hand; nevertheless, the past ten weeks, in return for the increase of her poise, had taken something from her vitality. Quickness of eye, firmness of hand, evenness of temper: all these may be gifts of the gods. Their use is a purely human function, and proportionately exhausting. The girl's one salvation lay in the fact that her quick sympathy with her patients was for the most part impersonal. Up to this time, Weldon had been her only patient whom she had known outside the routine duties of her hospital life. In a sense, it had been a relief to meet some one whom she knew to be of her own world; in a sense, the case had worn upon her acutely. She could watch with a greater degree of stolidity the sufferings of other men.

Among her new charges, that day, only one had made any distinct impression upon her overworked brain. That was a jovial young fellow, handsome as Phoebus Apollo, in spite of a slashing scar across one cheek. He had answered to her questions regarding his wounded foot with an accent so like that of Weldon that involuntarily she lingered beside him to add a word of cheery consolation. His was her final case, that night. As she wearily turned towards her own room, she made no effort to analyze her exhaustion.

She found Ethel, still in her hat and jacket, sitting on the edge of her own narrow cot.

"Cooee Dent!"

"Yes, dear." The girl's tone was nonchalant, even while the telltale color came into her cheeks.

"What are you doing here?"

"Visiting you, of course."

"Visiting me! But, Cooee, I really don't know where I can put you."

With perfect composure, Ethel passed her hand over the surface of the cot.

"Oh, I think this nutmeg-grater will carry two. Still, Alice, I must say that your hospitality isn't exactly exuberant."

Alice dropped into a chair and wearily pushed her hair still farther back from her forehead.

"But, Cooee--"

"Aren't you glad to see me?" Ethel demanded.

"Certainly. You are always a dear; but--I wish I had known you were coming."

Ethel raised her brows, and a slight edge came into her voice.

"If you don't want me, Alice, I can go home in the morning."

Dimly aware that her cousin was fencing with an invisible adversary, nevertheless Alice Mellen was too tired, that night, to range herself upon the side of that adversary. As far as she was concerned, Ethel had dropped upon her like a bolt from the blue. She was too busy, too absorbed in her patients to give more than a passing thought to even her most intimate cousin. And besides, Weldon--She pulled herself together sharply.

"Of course I want you, Cooee dear. It is only a bit sudden, and I am trying to think what to do with you."

Now and then Ethel turned wayward. This was one of the times.

"If you didn't know what to do with me, Alice, then why did you ask me to come?"

"But I didn't," Alice responded, too astonished to modify her denial into a polite form of fibbing.

Ethers tone was gently superior.

"Oh, yes; you did."

"When?"

"When you were leaving home. You said then that I must be sure to come up to spend a week with you, early in the winter." Then her accent changed. "You poor tired child!" she said, as she rose and crossed to her cousin's side. "This work is too hard for you; you look as if you had been fighting the Boers themselves, instead of merely enteric and bullet holes. I think it is just as well that I am here to look out for you, for a few days."

Alice lifted her hand to the hand that lay against her cheek.

"I am glad to see you, Cooee dear. I am only so surprised that it makes me slow to tell you so. If you can sleep here, to-night, I can find a better place for you in the morning."

"This will do," Ethel answered, while she slowly drew the pins from her hat. "It is neat, even if it isn't spacious. Really, Alice, I should have let you know; but it was only just as I was starting that I found I could come at all. Father is at home, and mother is unusually well, and I thought I would best make the most of the opportunity."

Crossing the room to the table, she stood with her back to her cousin, while she smoothed the feathers in her hat. Then, without turning, she asked abruptly,--

"How is Mr. Weldon?"

"Better."

"Out of all danger?"

"Yes. Not that he has been in much danger, anyway."

"Oh, I thought--"

Then silence fell.

Alice, meanwhile, was busy with a swift calculation. Five days, in these troubled times, for a letter to go from Johannesburg to Cape Town; five days since Ethel could have left Cape Town. And her one letter to Ethel since Weldon's arrival had been posted just three days before.

"How did you know Mr. Weldon was here?" she asked sharply.

Ethel's back was still turned towards her. Nevertheless, she could see the scarlet tide mounting to the ears and to the roots of the vivid gold hair.

"Why, your letter, Alice," Ethel answered composedly.

Alice's laugh was sharp and edged with malice.

"Yes, dear. My letter, telling you of his being here, will be delivered at your house to-morrow morning."

"Oh, then I must have mixed things up," Ethel replied, as she turned to face her cousin. "Probably Captain Frazer told me."

"Captain Frazer?"

"Yes, he came down to Cape Town, just before I left there. I remember now, he was the one who told me. He was near Mr. Weldon at Vlaakfontein; he knew all about his awful ride into Krugersdorp, and I believe he did say be was to be brought here."

For a moment more, the two pairs of eyes, the blue and the black, met in steady warfare, neither one yielding in the least, neither one quite aware how much she was betraying to the other.

"Well, what of it?" Ethel demanded tempestuously then.

"Nothing, only--are you sure you were wise to come?"

The blue eyes blazed.

"And what do you mean by that, Alice? You asked me to visit you here, to see your work among your patients. I have come. If I came at all, it had to be now. I can't always leave home for a week at a time. And I can't help it, can I, if Mr. Weldon happens to be one of your patients?"

"No; you can't," Alice admitted slowly. "It only remains to be seen whether you would care to help it, if you could."

Again Ethel crossed the room. This time, she dropped down at her cousin's side.

"Don't let us argue about it and get cross at each other, dear. If I have made a mistake in coming now, I am sorry. But I am here. Let me stay a few days; I may be able to help you a little. Anyway, I promise not to be a trouble to you. It is so long since I have seen you, Alice. And--" Again the silence dropped.

Alice roused herself from the reverie which was creeping over her. She was glad to see Ethel, unfeignedly glad. The bright, animated presence of her cousin, during the next few days, could not fail to be a tonic. And, as Ethel had said, she herself had been the one to suggest the first idea of the winter visit. Chance and Captain Frazer had decreed that it should take place now, when Alice's hands were immoderately full of work. But then, so much the better. Ethel could make herself invaluable among the convalescents. She herself had not put on her Red-Cross badge for the sake of taking her rest hour at the bedside of Trooper Harvard Weldon.

Half undressed, Ethel paused, hair brush in hand. "You can't imagine how tired I am, Alice. It is a terrible journey up here nowadays. I was in terror of a train-wreck at any moment," she said drowsily. "Don't let me sleep too long in the morning, because," she pulled open her eyes long enough to dart a mocking glance over her shoulder at her cousin; "because you know, right after breakfast, you are going to let me begin to help you take care of some of your people."

From behind her own sheltering veil of ink-black hair, Alice laughed.

"Cooee, you are a dear; but you're rather a trial," she said slowly. "However, now that you are here, I think I shall ask the P. M. O. to set you to work to watch over the needs of Mr. Weldon. He won't be here much longer; but, while he stays, I shall consider him your patient." Then, brushing aside the veil, she bent forward and touched her lips to her cousin's cheek.

"Might I ask what brought you up here, Miss Dent?" Weldon asked, the next day.

Beside him sat Ethel, her hands demurely clasped in the lap of her broad white apron.

"My cousin's invitation," she replied.

"Then Miss Mellen knew you were coming?"

"Yes. She asked me to come, early in the winter."

"Strange she said nothing about it! We were talking about you, only yesterday."

"She didn't know, even then, that I was so imminent," Ethel answered. "I took her quite by surprise, at the last."

"A surprise all around, then," he said, with a boyish laugh. "I was astonished to find Miss Mellen here, and you must have been equally astonished to find me. If only Captain Frazer would appear, our old quartette would be complete."

"I am afraid we must get on without him," she said lightly.

"Unfortunately, yes. I wonder where he is."

"In Cape Town," she replied unexpectedly.

"Really? What is he doing there?"

"Don't expect me to tell. It has something to do with a staff; but whether he carries it, or becudgels recruits with it, I have no idea at all."

"He hasn't left the Scottish Horse?"

"In fact; but not in name. Your regiment is still in the Transvaal; but he keeps a sort of vicarious connection with it. Please don't expect me to grasp military details, Mr. Weldon. I merely repeat the facts, parrot fashion; you must interpret them to suit yourself."

He laughed again. Already, in that one morning, he appeared to have taken a long stride towards the regaining of his old self.

"You are a perfect gazette, Miss Dent, the first bit of news that has crept inside this place. Where did you get all your information?"

"From Captain Frazer." Her rising color belied her unconcerned tone.

"You have seen him, then?"

"Yes. He is usually very good about calling, whenever he comes to Cape Town."

"And is he well?"

"Absolutely. Also quite enthusiastic over his troopers and the work they did at Vlaakfontein."

"Were--many--"

She understood.

"Not very many; but several were wounded. Worst of all, one or two of the wounded ones were shot by the Boers. Mr. Carew told me that he left a dozen of your men in the hospital at Krugersdorp."

"Carew? Have you seen him, too, Miss Dent?"

"Didn't you know he was here?"

He stared at her in blank amazement.

"Here in Johannesburg?"

"Here in this hospital."

"In what shape?"

"Hilarious in his mind, and with a foot that is coming out right in course of time. Didn't Alice tell you?"

"No."

"Strange. She took me to see him, this morning, on my way here, because he was such a promising patient. She was quite surprised to find we were old acquaintances."

"Oh," Weldon said slowly. "I begin to see. Miss Mellen had never met Carew, so she had no idea we were friends. What a curious snarl it all is!"

"The hand of Fate is in it," Ethel assented idly.

"Do you believe in Fate, too?"

"Surely. Why not?"

"Nothing, only your cousin said you didn't."

The girl frowned.

"Alice doesn't know all my mental processes," she said a little severely.

"She didn't pretend to. We were speaking of Fate, yesterday, of the way certain events in one's life seem absolutely inevitable; at least, I was. Then the conversation worked around to you, and Miss Mellen suggested that you usually rose superior to Fate," Weldon explained at some length.

Once again, Ethel felt the note of finality in his tone. For an instant, she shut her lips. Then she reverted to the main question.

"How do you mean inevitable?"

"As if you chose your path, and then found that, for always, it had been the only thing for you to do. That's not so clear, I know; but I can't put it much better."

"For instance?"

"For instance, my coming out here when I did. I was interested in the war; but there was no real question of my coming, until the month I sailed. Then, all of a sudden, I seemed to know why it was that I had spent my life on horseback. They told me in England that the real war was over. When I landed at Cape Town, I found out that the one thing needed was a man who could ride, and shoot straight. From the day I sailed from home, until now, I have been like an actor walking through a part that some one else has written for him. I have chosen nothing; it all has been inevitable."

She rose to her feet, and stood leaning on the back of her chair.

"In that case, Mr. Weldon, you must include our meeting in your scheme of things," she said, with a smile.

His answering smile met her smile with perfect frankness.

"I sometimes wonder if that wasn't the most inevitable part of it all."

CHAPTER TWELVE

The red-brown veldt stretched away to the sky-line, sixty miles distant. Level as it looked, it was nevertheless a succession of softly rolling ridges dotted with clumps of dried sagebrush and spotted here and there with heaps of black volcanic rocks. Far to the northward, a thin line of poplars and willows marked the bed of a river. Beyond that, again, the air was thick with smoke from acres of burning veldt. The days were full of dust, and the nights were full of frost; it was the month of June, and winter was upon the land.

The camp was taking a well-earned rest. For days, the men had swept over the veldt, following hard on the trail of a Boer general who only made himself visible now and then by a spatter of bullets, when his convoy train was delayed at a difficult ford. It had been a week of playing pussin-the-corner over a charred and dusty land, where the only roads were trails trodden out to powder by the hoofs of those that had gone before. Both men and mounts were wellnigh exhausted, and the officers had decreed a halt.

The strain had been intense. Now, with the relaxing of it, its memory vanished, and the halt swiftly took upon itself the appearance of a school holiday. Laughing and chaffing each other, groups of men loitered here and lounged there, smoking, writing letters, and taking stout, unlovely stitches in their time-worn khaki clothing. At one side of the camp was the tent of the mess sergeant, equipped like a portable species of corner grocery. Near by, Paddy apparently was in his element, presiding over his camp- kitchen, a vast bonfire encircled with a dozen iron pots. At the farther edge of the camp Weldon was umpiring a game of football between his own squadron and a company of the Derbys. Owing to the athletic zeal of the hour, it was big-side, and Weldon was too busy in keeping his eye upon so many players to pay much attention to his own loneliness.

In all truth, however, he was lonely. The week since he had rejoined his squadron had dragged perceptibly. Captain Frazer was in Cape Town; Carew was still in hospital at Johannesburg where, under the eyes of Alice Mellen and her cousin, he was fast resuming his old finical habits. Dingy and veldt-stained though he might be, Carew at heart would always remain the exquisite. However, exquisite that he was bound to be, he was even more the soldier, and his gay eyes had clouded, as he had wrung Weldon's hand in parting.

"Lucky dog!" he said enviously. "I am off duty for two weeks more, and you are going back to the thick of things. One must take it as it comes; but I say, old man, don't forget me when the bullets begin to pelt at you again."

And Weldon had been better than his promise. He had thought of Carew, day and night, for the entire week, thought of him and missed him acutely. Carew was an ideal comrade in that he never, under any circumstances, took himself in earnest.

A leg which will carry a man on horseback is by no means fit for football. Weldon, finished player that he was, found it tame work to umpire a team whose sole idea of tactics was to get there in any way that offered itself. Half an hour sufficed; then, appointing an understudy, he walked away in search of Paddy. From the midst of a torrent of instructions to his quartette of black subordinates, Paddy's voice sang out a cheery greeting.

"Come along, little feller! Come and get something to eat. It's hungry you ought to be, the day, after the way you've been walking all over the country on horseback and an empty stomach. Try this, as a sample of your dinner, and sit down by the edge of the fire, whilst, and tell me how it tastes."

The iron spoon scraped lustily over the iron dixey. Then Weldon returned them both with a low bow.

"Like yourself, Paddy, short and sweet."

Paddy brandished the spoon, weapon-wise.

"Short is it, you little Canuck! So is a pepperpot short; but it holds a hell of a flavor. Leave Paddy a gun in his hand, and his short legs will keep up with your long ones, when it's the firing line that's before him."

"The old sing-song, Paddy. Give us something new."

"So will I, when I get my wishing. Till then, you'll hear it over and over again. A man of my temper, little one, will never rest content at a firing line that's all surrounded about with ten-quart pots of boiling beef."

"Why don't you resign, then?"

"Resigned! How can I be resigned? I'm a chunk of dynamite in a suet- pot, hard to manage and ready to go off at any time that something strikes me. Meantime, I am like what they say is dirt: matter out of place."

"Then why don't you get out?" Weldon queried.

"I am out of place now, I'm telling you," Paddy returned, as he pensively rested his cheek upon the bowl of the spoon in his hand.

"Yes; but why not refuse to stay here as cook?"

Sorrowfully Paddy shook his head, spoon and all.

"That's what I did do, little one."

"And what happened?"

"This." The spoon came into evidence once more. "They blarneyed me up and they blarneyed me down, and they said nobody could cook like Paddy. Anybody could shoot a baker's dozen of Boers; but only one man in the camp could fill up the boys to give them a fit and level stomach for the battle. And here I am, and here I'm like to be, till the new moon in the heavens turns to a curly strip of bully beef. If I'd known the Captain was about to escape to Cape Town, it's Paddy that would have escaped with him, hanging on to the tail of his coat. Saint Patrick's vipers! What's that?"

A hum, a spat, and a little spurt of red dust rolled lazily upward. Then another hum followed. There was a scurry of men, a squeak of leather, the light clashing of rifles snatched from the stack; and the troops were off.

Beside them, the nearer hills rose in brick-red patches against the sky. Farther away, the brick color changed to gray and, still beyond, to misty purple. Before them rolled the open, khaki-colored veldt dotted in one direction by a ragged spot of black that flowed over the crest of each ridge and vanished from sight for a moment before rising from the hollow to flow over the crest of the ridge beyond. And towards the ragged spot of black there rushed onward, at an ever-lessening distance, the khaki-colored streak of the foremost rank of C Squadron, led for the moment by a little gray broncho whose hoofs touched the ground only to spurn it backwards.

The chase was long and hot; but the end was in sight. Directly across the path of the quarry stretched a low line of willows showing the course of the stream beneath, and, a few hundred feet this side of the willows, scattered clumps of green marked as many scattered dwellings. By the largest clump, the quarry halted and turned to bay, and the pursuers, unable to check their speed, rode down upon it and crashed through its ranks, regardless of the pitiless. fire, then, sweeping around on the arc of a mammoth circle, took up their position in the shelter of a walled kraal, only a few hundred yards away. Then for a moment they halted, face to face and in absolute silence.

Even after her mad race, the little gray broncho was breathing deeply and easily; but Weldon could feel his own breath come short. Banged in open order before him were a full half-hundred of the enemy, bearded, black-coated, bandoliered, grim and stolid and ripe of years. Beside him were the new captain of the troop and seven men. They were and alert; but there were only nine of them in all. And the rest of the troop, it seemed to him, were half the veldt-length away. Vaguely he wondered whether their distant khaki coats would look as purple as did the distant khaki-colored hills. Then, quite inconsequently, as he raised his rifle, he noticed that one of the Boers had a button hanging loosely on its threads from the front of his coat. He was rather surprised, the next instant, to see the Boer pitch forward headlong in the dust. It was some time afterward that he thought to connect the falling with the crack of his own rifle.

Piggie bounded sidewise, as the mount of the trooper next Weldon dropped and lay whimpering like a hurt child. Then she steadied to the touch of Weldon's hand upon her neck. It was not the first time he had guided her, unscathed, through a leaden shower. She would trust him yet once again. As he raised his rifle, her wiry legs were as steady as four iron rods. He saw another Boer fall and yet another and a third; but one khaki-colored figure lay stiffly beside him, and another was dragging itself away to a corner of the kraal, to give greater space to its unwounded comrades. And still the bullets whizzed about them, thick and ever thicker.

Piggie shied again. This time a bullet had grazed her neck, and the sight of the narrow sear filled Weldon's mind with a dull, unreasoning rage. Brutal to aim at the plucky mounts who bore their riders so gallantly into the flight where all defensive power was denied themselves! He paused long enough to pat the firm gray neck, to feel the answering pressure against his hand. Then he raised his rifle again and took careful aim, as he breathed a wordless prayer that chance might guide his bullet into the man who had scarred his faithful friend. Another Boer dropped; Weldon hoped it was by his own bullet. Then both he and the gray broncho pricked up their ears as, close on their flank, they heard the beating of galloping hoofs.

In the shock of the scrimmage that followed, there was scant time to take thought of friend or of foe. On the heels of his new captain as, of old, he had been on the heels of Captain Frazer, Weldon and the gray broncho were in the thick of the fight. Then, as the Boers sullenly fell backwards, Weldon became aware of a familiar voice in his ears.

"Whisht, little feller! It's Paddy," the voice said in a spooky undertone, as its owner ranged up alongside the gray broncho.

"Paddy!" Weldon stared at him in unfeigned astonishment. "What in the name of heaven are you doing here, man?"

With perfect composure Paddy squared himself in the saddle.

"Little Canuck dear, as I told you before, heaven is a state of eternal peace, and therefore an undesirable abode in these hot times. I prefer a whiff of brimstone, myself; and, by the powers, I've been getting, it." As he spoke, he took off his hat and showed a neat trio of holes in the left brim.

"But how did you come here, Paddy?" Weldon asked again.

"Took your advice to heart, my jewel, kicked over my pan of fat and jumped into the fire. Which, being put into straight English, I swiped a horse and rode off with the rest of the boys on the tail of the serpent." Weldon gasped, as he realized the enormity of the crime. Then he laughed. In his haste to gain possession of a mount, Paddy had taken no thought for his armament. His sole weapon was the huge iron spoon, still grasped in his left hand.

"Whose horse did you take, Paddy?"

"I d'know. I never looked to see. I popped my toe into the stirrup and came away, hot-foot; but," Paddy paused for a deliberate wink; "as I was leaving camp, I thought I heard the voice of that pigeon- toed little cockney Parrott, him that used to stub his toes on the wall at Piquetberg Road, acalling out that some one had mislaid his horse and he couldn't find it. I was sorry; but I was in a divil of a haste and couldn't stop to condole with him then."

"But, Paddy, they'll run you out of camp for this," Weldon remonstrated dutifully.

Paddy's shoulder mounted towards his left ear. "I'm thinking I have run myself out, and that's just what I was meaning to do. I've been a captain with four lieutenants under me. Any one of them can sling the pepper and the salt, and they're welcome; but not one has the fighting blood in his veins as I have. Let them mind their kettles and leave me to mind the enemy."

"And if they won't let you go back?"

"Then I'll ship myself straight down to Cape Town, and take service with Captain Frazer. He can fight with the best of them, and he knows I'm a man. It's riding at his heels I'll be, henceforth and forevermore."

Turning, Weldon looked long into the jovial Irish face, and at the hunchy figure that joggled to and fro in the saddle, with no heed to the rhythm of his horse's pace.

"Who taught you to ride, Paddy?" he asked at length.

For an instant, a lump in Paddy's left cheek betrayed the whereabouts of his tongue. Then quietly he made answer, "Sure, little feller, it must have been the grace of Saint Patrick. Nobody else has ever took a hand in the training of me. But I'll back him against all the riding masters in London and Aldershot."

And the result showed that Paddy's confidence was not misplaced.

CHAPTER THIRTEEN

By midwinter, the war had become a series of guerrilla raids, of sweeping drives and of occasional skirmishes. The epoch of the infantry had passed, and it was the day of the mounted man. The home-going of the great Field Marshal, six months before, had been followed by the return to England of transports loaded with foot soldiers. The hour, the country and the enemy all demanded the man on the horse. With Lord Kitchener in the field and the colonies aiding the mother country, the outcome was only a matter of time; but few could as yet say when the fulness of that time should be at hand.

"But it leaves me a good deal puzzled in my mind," Weldon said thoughtfully.

"How do you mean?" Ethel Dent threw the question at him a little defiantly.

"About going home."

"Surely, you aren't going now?"

He winced at the accent.

"I am not sure. I volunteered for six months. My time is up; I paid my official visit to the Citadel yesterday."

"Are you needed at home?"

"No. At least, not in any real sense."

"But you are needed here."

"There are enough without me, and the need will not last long."

"Don't be too sure. On the Dunottar Castle, there were plenty of people who laughed at you men for coming out to volunteer, after the war was over. You have proved that they laughed at nothing. Prove it again."

Rising, he walked the length of the room and stood looking out from the long front window. The bamboo screens and the willow chairs were gone from their veranda corner; the flower-boxes were empty now, and Table Bay gleamed coldly back at him in the late afternoon sun of midwinter. Then he turned around to face the girl, seated where her golden hair seemed to him to catch and hold all the light centering about the gay little tea-table.

"Don't," he said with some impatience. "Your arguments all echo my own wish. I am pulled in two ways at once. At home, the mother is growing restless. Since Vlaakfontein, she has lost her nerve, and her heart is set on my meeting her in London in October."

Deliberately Ethel made a neat triangle out of three unused spoons.

"Well?" she said, without looking up.

"Piggie and I have had a smell of powder," he answered briefly. "We want more."

"Well?" she said again.

"The question is, are we likely to get it."

"Not in England; not even in Cape Town," she answered, smiling at the spoons before her.

"Then where?"

"Wherever the Boers are thickest."

"Yes; but, after all, you are talking platitudes, Miss Dent," he said, with recurring impatience.

This time, she lifted her dark blue eyes to his face and allowed them to rest there for a full minute.

"But you forbade me to argue," she said demurely.

He dropped down into a chair and faced her resolutely.

"Now look here, Miss Dent, I can't talk shop in tea-table English. In fact, shop has no place at a tea-table, anyway. Still, you were the one to start it. Let's have it out. I don't want to funk, at this late day. If there is any fighting to be done, I want a hand in it. I went into a game of a certain length; I hope I played up, and stuck to the professional rules. That game is played out. I am not Trooper Weldon of the Scottish Horse. I am plain Harvard Weldon again and, to be quite frank, I don't like the change from khaki to tweed. But about going in for another game: it all depends on what the game will be. If it plays itself out, well and good; if it just dribbles on and on, without accomplishing anything, even an end, then I can see no use in going in for it. Fighting is one thing; having a picnic all over the face of South Africa is quite another matter. And, for the life of me, I can't see which is bound to come."

There was a minor cadence to the final phrase. Then he fell silent, and sat staring at the rug, while Ethel, leaning back in her chair, studied him at her ease. All in all, she was pleased with the result of her study. Always frank and likable, Weldon had developed wonderfully during those past months of hard work and slender comfort. Underneath his sunburn, his face had taken on new lines of resolution. His eyes were as clear as ever; but their boyishness was all in the past. It was a man who had come striding into the room, that afternoon, and paused beside her tea-table. And Ethel, looking up, had greeted him as she might have greeted Baden-Powell in his place.

To a great extent, Cape Town was resuming at least a semblance of its oldtime social life. Heroes were more plentiful than is altogether normal, however, and there was a dust-colored tint to most assemblages. During the past months, the Dents' house had come to be one of the focal points of society, and there were few men of note who had failed to mount the wide white steps and pass between the flanking pillars at the top, on their way to the drawing-room beyond. Once there, they usually came again, immediately, if they lingered in Cape Town; on their way back from the front, if no quicker opportunity offered itself. Many a bullet-interrupted conversation was resumed there; many a boy, just out from home, confided his mingled homesickness and aspirations to dainty, white- haired Mrs. Dent in her easy-chair; many a seasoned officer forgot his ambitions and his disappointments and even his still sensitive wounds in the gay talk of the golden-haired girl by the tray. As a rule, Ethel talked shop with no man. She merely looked sympathetic, and left him to do the talking, which he did unhesitatingly and without reservation. From the first hour of their meeting, Weldon had been the one exception. Even in the hospital at Johannesburg, she had gone over with him in detail his experiences in camp and field, and it had been Weldon by no means who had done all the talking.

To-day, as she had welcomed the tall Canadian in his irreproachable frock-coat, she had known a sudden pang of regret. Undeniably, his tailor was an artist. Nevertheless, she liked him better as she had seen him last, in his stained khaki and his well-worn shoes, bending over her hand in farewell, then taking The Nig's bridle from the waiting Kruger Bobs, to leap into the tarnished saddle, lift his hat and ride away out of sight. No one but Ethel herself had known that it was not distance alone which had rendered him invisible to her. And the next week in the hospital had dragged perceptibly. At the end of that time, she had been quite ready to say good by to Johannesburg and all that it contained. But, meanwhile, her smile gave no clue to her memories, as she offered her hand to Weldon.

"I knew you were here," she said cordially; "and I have any number of things to talk over with you. There is no talking for me now, though, with all these people on my hands. Can't you stay on and dine with us? That will give us an hour to gossip comfortably, and Captain Frazer is to be the only other guest. I asked him, on the chance of your appearing. Oh, good afternoon, Colonel Douglas!"

And Weldon found himself swept on out of her radius.

He took refuge beside Mrs. Dent and, from that safe slack-water, he made a thorough survey of the room. It was the first time he had been present at one of the Dents' reception days, and he acknowledged himself surprised at what he saw. Here and there an acquaintance nodded to him; but, for the most part, he was a stranger to the guests, save for the dozen whom he knew well by sight and better still by reputation. Moreover, while he watched her, he began to wonder whether he were not something of a stranger to Ethel herself. This stately girl was not the comrade with whom he had tramped the deck of the Dunottar Castle, nor yet the friend of his early days in Cape Town, nor yet again the blithe companion of his last tedious hours of convalescence. This girl was altogether admirable; but a bit awe-inspiring withal. He watched the non-chalant ease with which she provided a white-haired veteran of many wars and many orders with a cup of steaming tea, and then sat and chatted with him while he drank it. He felt himself a bashful boy, as he watched her, and, like any other bashful boy, he fell to talking to Mrs. Dent about his mother.

Then the last visitor made a reluctant exit, and Ethel crossed the room to his side. With the passing of the little throng of guests her assured manners had passed, and she met him with the same informal manner which had marked those last days at Johannesburg.

"Now," she said, as she dropped down beside her mother's chair; "you must tell me all about everything, Mr. Weldon. And, first of all, are you quite strong again?"

Question had followed question, eager, girlish and sincere, until Weldon's answers had covered all the interval since they last had met. At length, the delicate little mother had gone away to rest before time for dinner. Weldon's strong arm had half-supported, half-carried her up the staircase. Then, returning to the drawing- room, he had joined Ethel beside the deserted tea-table.

"After six months of the billy and the fryingpan, it is wonderfully good to handle china again," he said, as he halted on the hearth rug and stood smiling down at her.

She smiled back at him in full approval. Weldon looked very much the lord of creation, as he stood there with his back to the fire and one elbow resting on the mantel beside him. The position suited him, and, speaking in quite another sense, it suited her also.

"Then a taste of civilization is pleasant now and then, even to a grizzled warrior like yourself?" she questioned lightly.

"Yes, for the time being. One never knows, though, how long that time being will last."

"What shall you do, when the war ends?"

"Go home, take up a share in the pater's business, and grow stout and lazy," he answered her unsmilingly.

"An alluring prospect."

"Yes; but there will be other things: an occasional dinner, and even a tea now and then."

Leaning back in her chair, she looked up at him through her long yellow lashes.

"And shall you never remember to miss Africa?" she asked indolently.

His eyes rested upon her gravely.

"Yes, often. Moreover forgive my bluntness, but it is one of the privileges of a soldier--moreover, Miss Dent, I shall miss you."

Her color came; but she made no effort to ignore his words.

"Thank you," she said, with equal gravity. "I am glad to have you say so. But I hope it may be long before that day comes." "I can't tell. I had expected to sail for home, in a week or two. Now I am not so sure."

"Whether you wish to?"

"Whether I ought. When I left the Transvaal, the work seemed nearly done. Down here, the stories are less promising." He paused; then he added thoughtfully, "But it leaves me a good deal puzzled in my mind."

Coffee was served in the drawing-room, that night. Ethel roused herself from a reverie as Weldon and Captain Frazer joined her. To their half-mocking questions, she admitted the fact of her thoughtfulness. To neither one did she see fit to acknowledge its cause. The mood passed swiftly, however, and it left her more brilliantly gay than either man had ever seen her until then. Each frankly confessed himself dazzled; each one of them, more grave by nature than she often showed herself, was secretly uneasy lest her sudden overflow of spirits was in some fashion directed towards his companion; yet so skilfully did she lead the conversation that, at the evening's end, neither Weldon nor the Captain could produce any valid claim to being considered the favored guest.

"It has been good to have you here," she said gayly, as she gave them each a hand at parting. "Even if I was not present at your meeting, I have always felt that I had a finger-tip, at least, in your friendship." Then, as she dropped their hands, she faced the Captain with sudden seriousness. "Captain Frazer," she said slowly; "Mr. Weldon's time is over, and he has left the service. He thinks the fighting is all done. I am only a woman; I can't explain things very clearly, and so," she hesitated a little; "and so I think I shall leave his soul in your hands. There are plenty of people still in South Africa; there are never too many men." And, with a grave little nod, half intent, half girlish, she turned away from the door, leaving the heavy drapery to sway to and fro behind her.

CHAPTER FOURTEEN

Three days later, Weldon ran lightly up the stone steps and rang at the Dents' door.

"Is Miss Dent in?" he asked the maid. "I know it isn't her day; but tell her I am leaving town almost immediately, and I wish to say good by."

Notwithstanding his message, Ethel was long about appearing, and her face and manner, when she halted on the threshold, were a bit unapproachable. Then, as her eyes lighted on the brown uniform and the wide slouch hat, her whole expression changed, and she came forward with an eagerness which she was at no pains to conceal.

"Mr. Weldon."

He bowed in mock humility.

"Trooper Weldon, if you please."

"I am delighted. Is it your old troop?"

He shook his head.

"No. I know the Transvaal and all its resources by heart. I have chosen the Orange Free State. It is a new country; and, besides, all the best of the fighting is going to be there, on the heels of De Wet."

"Are you a prophet?" she asked, while she dropped into a chair and motioned to him to be seated.

"No; but I suspect that Captain Frazer is," he answered, as he obeyed her.

She raised her brows questioningly.

"Does he go, too?"

"Not now. His staff work holds him here among the fleshpots," he replied." Later, he may be able to come up to us."

"Us?"

"The South African Light Horse."

"Why did you choose them?"

"Because they are to operate in the Orange River country, and because they would have me."

"Is that a matter to consider?"

Weldon laughed while, placing his hat on the floor, he settled himself more comfortably in his chair. His face was unusually animated, that day, and his trim new uniform and his carefully-wound putties added inches to his height and showed his lithe, lean figure at its very best.

"I considered it," he answered then. "It is a trick of mine, as soon as I decide I want a thing, to be in living terror of losing it. However, the ordeal was short and not too severe. Captain Frazer introduced me to a little lieutenant who looked me over, asked me if I could ride, if I could shoot a rifle and if I had had any experience. I fancy the matter was settled beforehand. Then I went out and treated The Nig and Piggie to some new shoes, and myself to a new uniform, and the deed was done."

"Are you glad, or sorry?" she asked slowly.

"That there was no more red tape?"

"That you decided as you did?"

He stared at her thoughtfully for a minute. Then he answered,--

"But I imagine it rather decided itself. I spoke of it to you once before, I remember, when we were up in hospital, how there never seemed to be much choice open to me. I fancy I am deciding things; I mull over them till I am disgusted with the whole matter. Then, after I have made up my mind what I am going to do, I suddenly realize that there was never any question about it from the start. I have simply said 'yes' to an irresistible force."

"Perhaps," she assented slowly. "I am not so sure." Then she turned to the tangible fact. "But when do you go?"

"To-morrow morning."

"I am sorry it must be so soon," she said quietly. "Still, I am glad you are going. You never would have been satisfied to sail for home now."

"No," he answered. "I should not."

Then the talk halted again.

"Where is Mr. Carew?" she asked abruptly at length, less from interest in Carew than from a desire to escape so insistent a pause.

"At the Mount Nelson." "Here in Cape Town?"

"Yes. He came down with me. We volunteered together, you know, and his time was ended, too."

"Does he go home?"

"No; not Harry Carew. We had decided to keep together in our plans; in fact, it was one of the conditions of our coming out. But, from the start, he has hated the idea of going back home as long as there was an armed Boer left in the field."

"And he goes with you?"

"Yes, to Springfontein. We have our headquarters there for the present. For Carew's sake, I hope it will be more riding and scouting than actual fighting. The man is made of some material that draws all the bullets in sight."

Ethel smiled.

"Don't let him stop near you, then," she advised.

"Why not? He is as good as a shield. It is hard on him, though. He was hit four or five times before Vlaakfontein, and has had one scratch since."

"What is the trouble? Is he foolhardy?"

"Foolhardy in war, Miss Dent?"

"Yes, just that. There is no sense in taking needless risks."

"But it is mighty hard to draw the line between avoiding needless risks and funking necessary ones," he answered. "But Carew isn't reckless. He is plucky, but very level-headed, and he means to take care of himself, when he can. One can't always, you know. And then he is wonderfully unlucky."

"You believe in luck, then?"

"Yes, or Fate. What else makes a man move out of the way, just in time for the bullet to graze his cheek? He doesn't see the bullet coming; neither does the man who stops it. Both of them are busy about something else. For the man who escapes it, it is Providence; for the man who gets killed, it is Fate."

She tried to rouse him from his sudden gravity.

"And for both, it is mere chance."

"If you call it that. Miss Dent--" He hesitated.

"Yes," she assented gravely.

"It was only a chance, but a strange one," he went on, with his eyes fixed on the topmost ridge of his brown puttie. "We were climbing the face of a kopje, one day. It was very steep, and we crawled up a narrow trail in single file. Two days before, our guns had been shelling the whole kopje, and they must have cracked it up badly. All at once, the man above me loosened a great lump of rock. I was exactly underneath it. It gave a little bound outward, went completely over me and struck full on the head of the next man in line."

The girl sat, bending forward in her chair, her strong, quiet hands clasped loosely in her lap.

"And he?" she asked quite low.

"He dropped to the foot of the kopje, dead. In his fall, he dragged down the next man after him, and his leg was crushed."

"And you were saved!" she said a bit breathlessly.

"Doesn't it make you feel a vague responsibility, as if you must live up to something that you couldn't quite understand?"

Without looking up, he bowed in assent.

"Yes," he said then. "Don't think me foolishly superstitious, Miss Dent, or too egotistic. I try not to pay much attention to it. Once in a while, though, not too often, it all comes back over me, and I feel then as if my life might have been kept for something that is still ahead of me."

"And doesn't it leave you feeling anxious about making all your decisions?" she asked slowly, as she leaned back again in her chair.

"At first. Then I remember how that, and some other things have been settled for me."

"What then?"

"Then I shut my teeth and face forward. All one can do, is to forget the future and take the present as it comes, making the best of each minute and leaving the hour to look out for itself," he answered simply. "Sometimes one makes better progress by drifting than he does by punting against the current."

She bit her lip.

"Sometimes I think, though--" Suddenly she roused herself and gave a nervous little laugh. "Captain Frazer is coming up the steps," she added.

"You think?" Weldon reminded her, as she rose.

But she shook her head and laughed again, this time more in her natural manner.

"I think that I wish you would bring Mr. Carew to call on me, next time you come," she said evasively.

"Thank you. He will be glad to come. The only question is when the next time will arrive."

"You said Captain Frazer was a prophet," she said, as she moved towards the door. "Ask him."

Tall, alert, eager, the Captain entered the room in time to catch her words.

"A prophet of what and to whom, Miss Dent?" he asked, as he bowed over her outstretched hand.

"To Mr. Weldon, in regard to the future fighting," she answered gayly.

"You here, Weldon?"

"Yes, to say good by."

Captain Frazer nodded.

"I saw Mitchell, this morning. He spoke well of you; of Carew, too, for the matter of that. He told me your troop would be off in the morning, and asked me to diagnose ,your best points."

"Could you find any?" Weldon asked imperturbably. "A few. I told him you could sit tight and shoot straight," the Captain answered, laughing. Then he added gravely, "And I also told him you could ride the fiend incarnate, and that, as far as I knew, you didn't lose your head when you were under fire."

For the instant, Weldon forgot his hostess, as he looked up to meet the Captain's blue eyes squarely.

"Thank you. But it is more than I deserve."

"Then you must try to live up to it," Ethel advised him languidly. "It merely increases your responsibilities, for now you have two reputations to support, your own for pluck and the Captain's for being a judge of his fellowmen. It is an awful weight that you are carrying on your shoulders, Mr. Weldon."

"If it grows too heavy, I will slide some of it off on your own," he returned, as he picked up his hat and rose to his feet. "Your responsibility is back of mine, Miss Dent. It was you who advised me to stay in South Africa."

"Not at all. I presented the case and kept my advice to myself," she rebelled promptly.

"Certain presentments are stronger than much advising."

"Perhaps. But in the end, you remember, I commended your soul to Captain Frazer's keeping."

He bowed with the odd, old-fashioned deference which it pleased him to assume at times. "Captain Frazer may have saved it; but it may have been you who made it worth his efforts at salvation."

She laughed again. Nevertheless, her eyes showed her pleasure.

"Then we, Captain Frazer and I, must divide the responsibility for your future," she replied. "In any case, may it be all good!"

The drapery fell backward over his departing figure, and, for an instant, Ethel stood staring at the swaying folds. Then, turning, she walked back to the fire.

"All good," she repeated. "I know you echo the wish, Captain Frazer. But--isn't it hard to say good by?"

"In these days most of all," he assented slowly. "And one never can tell when his own turn may come."

"Nor what its end may be," she added. Then impetuously she rose again and moved up and down the room. "Look at that sunshine outside, Captain Frazer," she said restlessly. "It ought to forbid any such gloomy moods. I believe all this war and so many partings are spoiling my nerve. I really feel quite blue, to-day; and Mr. Weldon made it worse."

"By saying good by?"

Glancing up, she was astonished at the wishful, hungry look in the blue eyes before her. "Yes, a little," she said lightly; "for I hate the very word. But, if it must be spoken, it should always be short and staccato. Instead, he sat here, and we talked about Fate and wounds and all sorts of direful things." She shook herself and shivered slightly. Then she sat down in the chair which Weldon had just left vacant. "It is bad manners to have nerves, Captain Frazer. Forgive me first, and then tell me something altogether flippant, to make me forget things."

But her mood had caught the Captain in its grasp.

"Are you sure you want to forget?" he asked her gravely.

"Yes," she made vehement answer. "Always!"

But not even her decided answer brought back the eager light into his dark blue eyes.

Nevertheless, an hour later found him still sitting there. Ethel's depression had vanished, to be followed by a mood of wayward merriment for which the honest, straightforward soldier was totally at a loss to account. Sincere himself, he looked for sincerity in others. If Ethel's gravity had been unfeigned, how could it so soon give place to her present buoyancy? Not the strictest code of hospitality could demand that a hostess should straightway toss aside the thought of the parting guest who had gone away to battle and, perhaps, to sudden death. And, if the girl had been insincere in her parting from Weldon, why should she be sincere in her present absorption in his own interests? And, if her regrets for Weldon were as great as they had seemed to be, then what was the use of his remaining by her side any longer? The horns of the dilemma extended themselves to infinity and branched again and again as they extended. Meanwhile, his eyes were full of trouble, and his answers to her questions were vague and faltering. Until her sudden trip to Johannesburg, Captain Frazer had taken the girl as a matter of course. Since then, he had begun to doubt, and the doubts were thickening.

But, after all, there was no real reason for doubt. During her one short season in London, the Captain had met Ethel constantly, he had been quite obviously the favorite of the old aunt who had presided over the girl's introduction to society, and his later meetings with Ethel at sundry week-end gatherings had convinced him that he had no serious rival. Then had come the war; and Ethel's absence from town had made a farewell impossible. Captain Frazer had sailed away, leaving the past behind him; but the future was still his, to be lost or won, according to the use he made of his manhood's chances.

And then, on the dazzling summer morning which had ushered in the new century, he had caught a glimpse of Ethel riding towards home. Three days later, as he had gone away down the broad white steps, he had felt convinced that the future already lay in his grasp. It had been the selfsame Ethel, unchanged and changeless to his loyal mind, who had met him with smiling, eager cordiality. The year of separation was cast aside; their friendship began again at the precise spot where it had been broken off.

Since then, he had seen her often, occasionally alone, sometimes with her mother, sometimes the central figure of a little crowd who were obviously striving to win her favor. Her father's fortune was in part the cause of this; but the greater, surer cause lay within the girl's own personality. Ethel Dent was no negative character. However, Captain Frazer had never found her too absorbed in her other companions to be able to give him a share of her attention which differed from all other shares that she bestowed, in being a bit more personal in its cordiality. His black-fringed blue eyes were keen and far-sighted. They assured him that, whatever her regard for him, at least it was true that, in all her Cape Town life, there was no man for whom Ethel Dent had a sincerer liking. And then, all at once, a doubt had assailed his mind, and the doubt had centered itself in this long, lean Canadian with the grave, steady face and the boyish manner. Worst of all, the doubt had scarcely arisen before he himself had become aware of his own growing liking for the young Canadian. Captain Leo Frazer was strictly just. He admitted to himself that Weldon was in every way worthy to be chosen by Ethel Dent. However, he was determined as well as just, and he had no mind at all to allow Ethel Dent to choose any man but one, and that one was himself, Leo Frazer.

And now he was sitting moodily by her fireside, listening to her light, easy flow of talk and asking himself certain questions, which he was powerless to answer.

As he rose at last, some sudden impulse made him speak from the very midst of his train of thought.

"Did you know he had refused a commission?" he asked, regardless of antecedents.

She made no pretence of misunderstanding him.

"No. Did he?"

"Yes. Mitchell told me, this morning."

"I wonder why."

"He said he had pledged himself to stay with the rank and file, that it was easier to take orders than to give them."

"Strange!" she said thoughtfully.

"Strange that he should feel so?"

She shook her head.

"No. He told me about that, coming out. I am not surprised. But it is strange that he shouldn't have spoken of the matter now."

"It was like him. He doesn't tell all his best deeds," Captain Frazer said, with direct frankness "Still, I thought it was fairer that you should know."

Her color came, as she met his eyes; but she offered no question in regard to the meaning of his final phrase.

CHAPTER FIFTEEN

"Good reason they call them kopjes," Carew grumbled scornfully, as he swept his arm about the encircling landscape. "Every flat-top hill is an exact copy of every other flat-top hill, and they all are more or less hideous to behold. My one source of rejoicement lies in the fact that the pattern was worn out down here, instead of being sent up to make our mountains by. I hate a bobtail horse; but it's nothing so bad as these everlasting bobtail hills. And, by Jove, there comes another dust devil!"

Far away across the veldt, a tiny spurt of dust twirled up into the air and came spinning towards them like a huge, translucent top. Gaining momentum as it spun along and picking up more dust as it advanced, it came whirling onward, rising high and higher until it swept down on them, a huge, khaki-colored, balloon-like mass. It caught them in its whirl, ground its stinging, sifting particles into their clothing, their skin and even into their shut eyes. Then it passed them by, and went spinning away in its course. Carew swore softly, as he wiped the dust from his lashes.

"Beastly things! There really ought to be a society formed for the suppression of dust devils in their infancy. What do you suppose becomes of the things, Weldon? There's no stopping them, once they get under way; and, at their rate of growth, they could bury a township in their old age."

"Granted they could find one to bury," Weldon returned. "Meanwhile, observe your bath tub."

Carew glanced down at the dust-filled buckets at his feet.

"Oh, hang!" he said concisely. "And I was about to prink."

"One would think you needed it now more than ever," Weldon answered, as he shook himself free from the thickest of the dust. "What's the use of trying to keep clean, Carew?"

"Precious little. I used to talk about I 'the un-tubbed.' Now I mean, merely for the sake of example, to shave twice in the month, and swab myself off between whiles. It's not for comfort, I assure you. It's my belief that an occasional bath is worse than none. It merely stirs up memories of the buried past, and aspirations that can't be fulfilled. However--" And Carew, the quondam exquisite, pulled off his socks and shirt, punched them down into one of the buckets and then did his British best to wash himself in the other.

His lamentations rose again, however, when he put on his time- stained uniform once more.

"I now understand why Brother Boer sleeps in his clothes," he observed grimly. "Cleanliness, may be next to godliness; but it is mighty near the edge of the diabolical to put yourself back into clothes that are only fit for the dust bin. When I am field marshal of a long campaign, my first act will be to establish swimming tanks and laundries as a branch of the Army Service Corps. Meanwhile, see here!" His open hand came down on his dust-colored coat. Ten minutes later, the print of every finger was still distinctly visible.

Weldon watched him sympathetically. Thanks to the efforts of Kruger Bobs, his own clothing was slightly less filled with dust, and his abandoned socks came back to him in a state of comparative cleanliness. Satisfied with the fact, he made no effort to inquire into the method of its achievement.

Carew, meanwhile, his coat off, his sleeves rolled to his elbows, was grappling with his efforts to produce laundry effect from a wooden bucket and a few quarts of dingy water. Beyond splashing his putties and giving himself a pain in the hinges of his back, he accomplished little. The garments were very wet; but their griminess was increased, rather than diminished. Carew's face fell, as he lifted them one by one. Then he shook his head.

"They certainly aren't cleaner; but they may be a bit fresher for being irrigated," he observed hopefully. "Look out!"

Weldon dodged out of range, as a sock, squeezed from the ankle downward, yielded up its irrigation in a sudden spurt through the toe.

"Hold on, Carew; I'm no candidate for baptism," he adjured his friend. "Let your things soak for a while, and I'll send Kruger Bobs over to take them in hand, as soon as he gets through polishing off The Nig."

Carew straightened his aching back.

"I'll change work with him," he suggested promptly. "A horse is on your own level; it's degrading to run a Chinese laundry."

Weldon glanced from the wooden bucket to the soaked wrists and splashed putties of his companion.

"I wish Miss Mellen could see you now, Carew," he remarked unkindly.

With unexpected suddenness, Carew mounted his dignity.

"Unfortunately Miss Mellen is at Johannesburg. Moreover, Miss Mellen has probably seen men in this mess before now," he answered a little shortly.

"Doubtless. She may have been in a similar fix, herself. If she were, I suspect she would put it through and come out on top," Weldon replied, with an accent of hearty and respectful admiration which mollified his companion. "There's my call. I must go to inspect my day nursery." And, leaving Carew beside his amateur wash- tub, he went striding away to the farther side of the camp where a hollow between the hills had been converted into a monstrous kraal. Involuntarily he smiled, as he walked off to his duty. Carew had been an edifying spectacle, as he had sacrificed himself upon the altar of cleanliness. He had been neither deft, dignified nor devout; and, in all truth, Alice Mellen would have found it hard to recognize her finical patient in the dusty, unshaven man whose hair bore unmistakable signs of having been pruned with a pair of pocket scissors. Little of Carew's past month had been spent in the base camp at Springfontein. With hundreds of other men, he had gone galloping up and down the Free State on the slippery heels of De Wet, now being shot at by prowling Boers, now engaged in a lively skirmish from which he never made his exit totally unscathed, now riding for weary, dusty miles upon a scent which ultimately proved to be a false one. And, meanwhile, not a postbag came into camp without a letter for Carew, bearing the mark of Johannesburg. It was not altogether resultless that Carew's foot had been obstinately slow in its healing.

To Weldon, a fixture in camp, fell the care of receiving Carew's mail. At last, when one day the bag brought in two letters addressed in the same dashing, angular handwriting, he forsook his principles and made open comment.

"There is a slight monotony about your mail, in these latter days, Carew," he observed dispassionately. And Carew had answered, with perfect composure,--

"Yes, in view of my chronic trick of being potted at, I find it wise to keep on good terms with my nurse. It may prove handy in case of accident, like an insurance policy, you know. Is that all?" And, cramming the letters into his pocket, he walked away to his tent.

And Weldon, as he watched him, nodded contentedly to himself. He liked Carew; he also liked Alice Mellen. Beyond that, he made no effort to go. Just now, he cared to penetrate the thoughts of but one woman. The others he was willing to take on trust. Nevertheless, it would have caused him some surprise, could he have reviewed all the mental processes of Alice Mellen, during the past ten months. For Weldon, the days at Springfontein differed not one whit, one from another, yet each day was full of an excitement which sent his blood stinging through his veins. Every man in the regiment could ride a broken horse; but, for many of them their attainments stopped there, and broken horses were few and far between. With the increasing need of troopers for the guerrilla raiding into which the war was degenerating, with the inevitable losses of a long campaign, mounts of any kind were scarce. Nevertheless, consternation had descended upon the camp, one day, when three hundred kicking, squealing American bronchos had been detrained and placed at their service. The next day, casualties were frequent; on the day after that, there was made announcement that mounted parade would be omitted. Weldon read the notice, smiled and went in search of his captain. He was tired of inaction, and he felt his muscles growing soft. They hardened speedily, however.

Day after day, he went striding into the kraal whence, after a skirmish which was more or less prolonged, he emerged astride a mount which, with shrieking voice and rampant hoofs, gave notice to all that such a liberty could not be permitted. Nevertheless, it was permitted. Sometimes, the final contest took place miles away from the point of its beginning. Sometimes horse and rider settled the matter in the course of a few concentric circles of an hundred-yard radius; sometimes it bucked; sometimes it rolled, and sometimes it merely sat down upon its haunches, dog-wise, and refused to budge. Almost invariably, it came out from the contest, unscarred save for its dignity and its temper. Weldon's lips shut tight; but his eyes rarely blazed. These wild, frightened creatures taxed his patience and his resource; but they hardly touched his temper in the least.

"What's the use of thrashing a beast that's mad with terror?" he answered one critical amateur who had watched the game from a safe distance. "The creature is in a funk, as it is; there's no use in adding to it. All I'm after is to teach 'em that saddles and bridles don't bite. Treat 'em decently and sit tight, and they'll come right and learn to trust you in the end."

And, as mount after mount was delivered over to the waiting authorities, it came to be a matter of general belief that the regimental rough-rider knew his business, albeit he accomplished it more by dint of urging than by many blows. Six weeks of this work had told upon him, told in the right direction. Under the brown skin, the muscles stood out like knotted cords; his nerves were steady; he ate like a wolf and slept the dreamless sleep of a healthy child. To the outward eye, his face changed but little. Its outlines were more rugged, the curves of his lips a bit more resolute; but that was all.

Now and then, amid the merry group at the camp fire, he sat silent, while he let his mind range away to the southward. Somewhere there, in the green-ringed town in the mountain's shelter, was a tall girl with yellow hair and eyes which matched the zenith when it darkens after the dropping of the sun. His fancy painted her in every conceivable situation: walking, riding, resting at noonday in the shaded western end of the veranda, or pouring tea for relays of thirsty guests. As a rule, the Captain's figure was in the background of these pictures, and Weldon was content to have it so. In all South Africa, these were his two best friends; it was good that they could be together. And the Captain was an older man, much older. When one lives in the open air during twenty-four hours of every day, jealousy has scant place in his mind. The smaller vices are for the cramped town, not for the limitless, unbroken veldt.

And now and then a day brought with it a letter, frank, friendly and full of news. Those days Weldon marked with a white stone; but his sleep, on those nights, was as quiet and dreamless as ever. Facts were facts. Theories and hopes were for the future; and no man looks much to the future in a time of war.

Besides the letters, there were minor events, too, events which went to fill up the letters of reply. Now it was a hospital train which halted at the camp on the way southward, and each red-taped nurse had reminded him of Alice Mellen, and of those last days in Johannesburg. Now it was a two-day trek, as escort for a convoy train whose long lines of bullock-drawn wagons marked the brown veldt with a wavering stripe of duller brown. Again a wounded picket came straying back to camp, bleeding and dazed, to report the inevitable sniping which furnished the running accompaniment to most other events; or an angry squad came riding in, to tell of the shots which had followed close upon the raising of the white flag, or of the score of armed men who had suddenly leaped out from the safe shelter of a Red-Cross ambulance. And, on one occasion, he had been in the thick of a similar fray. Hand to hand, he had fought on the doorsteps of a farmhouse to which he and his five comrades had been bidden by a sprightly Boer in gown and sunbonnet. At the door, the bonnet had been cast from the cropped head, and the gown had been pushed back to give access to the bandolier beneath, while a dozen shots from an upper window had driven them from the dooryard into the comparative shelter of the lower rooms. The skirmish had ended with a charge up the stairway. Weldon, that same night, had written to Ethel a wholly humorous account of the whole affair, and it was not until long afterwards that she had learned from Carew, who had been of the party, which was the trooper who had mounted guard over the room where the aged grandmother had tucked herself away under her bed. The old Dutch vrouw had bidden him to share her shelter; but he had taken note of her dimensions, and had declined her hospitality. Later on, when the fight was over and she had painfully wriggled her way out from her trap, he had also declined certain of her manifestations of gratitude. Even chivalry to the aged possesses its humorous side.

Then, one November night, Weldon came into his tent with alert step and glowing eyes. He found Carew going through his camp outfit in detail, and, squatting on the floor in the corner, Kruger Bobs was cleaning accoutrements as if his life depended on it.

"You look as if events were about to happen," he observed, from the dispassionate distance of the doorway.

"They are."

"Ask them to include me, then."

"What do you need of events, you regimental broncho-buster?"

"One gets sick of even the best horseflesh in time," he answered nonchalantly.

"Sorry, for you are doomed to more of it."

"Another herd of bronchos?" Weldon's voice showed that the idea displeased him.

"No; but a two-hundred-mile trek across country."

"Good. I am tired of being cooped up, and a spin of that kind will be a boon."

Carew settled back on his heels and looked up at him.

"Spin is it! Your only spin will be on your own axis. We are to act as escort for a convoy train of fifty wagons and ten times fifty mules. We shall make six miles a day, and our tongues will be wholly corrupted by the language of the mule-drivers. And, in the end, we shall get to--"

"A glorious fight, I trust," Weldon supplemented.

Gloomily Carew shook his head. "No; merely to Winburg. We are going to provision Weppener and Ladybrand, and then make for the railroad again. We'll strike it at Winburg most likely. It is an unholy sort of hole, and I hear that the hotel serves watered ink and currant jelly under the name of claret. We shall sit there and sip it, until the train arrives, and then we shall entrain and come back again. And this," he emphasized his words by plumping forward on his knees once more; "and this is war!"

"Yes; but it lets us out on a longer leash than I have had for some time,"

Weldon said serenely. "Anyway, it is well for you that it is not likely to be a bloody campaign, for you'll be headed straight away from Johannesburg, and I misdoubt me if Winburg holds a hospital."

"Judging from my past records, it will have to found one, then," Carew answered composedly. "If I have to go through two hundred miles of the enemy's country, they might as well open up, in readiness for my coming. But what is the letter, old man?"

"News. Yours had knocked it out of my mind, though. Mine comes off later. Captain Frazer has been transferred to the South African Light Horse, and will come up here as adjutant, on the first."

Carew's face brightened.

"That's good hearing. He will be higher still, before De Wet is taken." "I hope so. Anyway, he is coming to us. Think of having him about again!"

"Much good will it do us! An adjutant doesn't mess with the trooper."

"Frazer will stick to his friends."

"Mayhap. Still, better men than he have gone dizzy, as they went up the ladder, and dizziness makes people look at what's above them, rather than at what is below," Carew answered oracularly. "Frazer's influence will be sound, and we shall feel it from one end of things to the other. Aside From that, we aren't likely to be much affected by his coming. Did Miss Dent tell any other news?"

"As it happens, Miss Dent didn't tell me this."

"Who, then?"

"Captain Frazer, himself," Weldon answered, with a quiet relish of his own victory. "He sends messages and all that to you." Then he added, "And who else do you think is coming?"

"With him?"

"Yes."

Carew shook his head.

"I've no idea, unless Lord Kitchener is about to pay us a visit. There were rumors of it, a week or so ago."

"Guess again. It's a mightier than Lord Kitchener, this time."

"Can't be."

Weldon laughed. "It is, for it is a man trained to two weapons, who has beaten his kettles into a helmet and his pepper-pot into a cartridge-box."

"Paddy?"

"Yes, Paddy. The Captain writes that he is thirsting for gore and glory, and that he has learned to ride anything from a clotheshorse to a nightmare."

Carew laughed.

"Paddy all over. He never could take things as they came."

"Except Parrott's horse," Weldon suggested.

"How did he get out of that scrape?"

"Went out. There was talk of official vengeance; but Paddy vanished, that same night. A week later, he turned up at the Captain's room in Cape Town, with a bundle of clothes and a story that was as leaky as a sieve. The Captain sent him out to Maitland to be licked into shape, and this is the result."

"No," Carew objected in a sudden burst of prophecy. "Mind my words, Paddy has not resulted yet. That will come, later on in the game."

CHAPTER SIXTEEN

Winburg may have all the elements of greatness; but greatness itself is lacking. Nevertheless, after watching a convoy train tool along over the green-flecked yellow veldt at the rate of six miles a day, after seeing nothing but an occasional isolated farmhouse, the little town appeared like a centre of civilization and excitement to the bored troopers, as they rode up the main street and pitched camp on the western edge of the town. There they sat and idly wondered behind which particular hill was the largest commando. No type of boredom is more acute than that which links itself with periods of inaction in the army. Fifteen minutes would have sufficed to exhaust the resources of Winburg; the troopers remained there for fifteen days. Only Kruger Bobs was fully in his element. His daily grooming of the broncho and his master once over, his time was his own, and he employed it to the best of his ability. Fate had endowed Kruger Bobs with a smile which won instant liking and gained instant fulfilment of his wishes. Just as, months before, he had sat on the river bank at Piquetberg Road, and grinned persuasively at the jam tins, so now he ranged up and down among the farms scattered about Winburg, and grinned himself into possession of manifold eggs and plump fowls and even of soft wheat bread, the final luxury of the biscuit-sated trooper who owned his fealty.

"'Is thy servant a dog?'" Carew had quoted gravely at sight of his first army biscuit.

And Weldon had made answer,--

"Not if he knows it. I have always had full sympathy with my hound who leaves his dog-bread in favor of a bit of oak planking gnawed out from his kennel floor."

But Carew was less dainty. Nevertheless, he attacked the biscuit with two flat stones, and mixed the debris with his coffee.

Now, however, thanks to the efforts of Kruger Bobs, they were living thriftily and upon the fat of the land.

"How do you get it all, Kruger Bobs? "Weldon had demanded, one day. "To my sure knowledge, you've no money, and people hereabouts don't love the British. What is your secret?"

Kruger Bobs ducked his bristly head into his ragged hat, and gave an explosive chuckle. Then he raised his head and scratched it demurely.

"Kruger Bobs just gits it, Boss," he explained comprehensively.

He came in, the next night, his pockets stuffed, his mouth wide ajar and the very whites of his eyes full of mystery. Carew and Weldon, sitting together, glanced up as he appeared. Instantly, as he caught sight of Carew, Kruger Bobs veiled his emotion and sought to become properly nonchalant. Nevertheless, it was plain that he had tidings to impart; and at length, over the top of Carew's head, he fell to making graphic, yet totally unintelligible, signs to his master.

"What in thunder do you want, Kruger Bobs?" Weldon demanded.

Kruger Bobs heaved an ostentatious sigh, cast at Weldon one flashing grin, and then asked dolorously,--

"Me speak Boss out dere?"

"What under heaven is the matter with you, Kruger Bobs?" Weldon asked, as he departed on the heels of his serving man.

Kruger Bobs slapped his thigh noiselessly, vanished behind his smile, then reappeared to put his lips to Weldon's ear and whisper in raucous triumph-- "Syb down dere Winburg."

"What? Who is Syb?" Weldon queried blankly.

Kruger Bobs straightened, in dignified resentment at his master's ignorance.

"Syb be my vrouw soon."

"Oh, I see. No wonder you look elated, you rascal. So you have been courting?"

The grin reappeared. "Ya, Boss. More, too."

"What now?" "Kruger Bobs got despatch from Syb for Boss."

Weldon's face expressed his amusement.

"Much obliged to the lady. Give her mine." "Syb say--" Again the thick black lips approached Weldon's ear, and the bristly head nodded energetically in time to the moving lips.

"Who?" Weldon said incredulously. "Miss Mellen?"

"Ya, Boss."

"How does Syb--Is that what you call her?--how does she know? Oh, I remember now. It is the girl who served at Miss Mellen's home," Weldon said, as light began to dawn.

"Ya, Boss; dat Syb."

"And she is here with Miss Mellen?"

Kruger Bobs nodded.

"What are they doing?"

"Dey is nurses sick mens." "How long have they been here?"

"One, tree, five day."

"Five days," Weldon translated to himself. "It was an odd chance, your running on her so soon. Did she know we were here?"

"She tink ya," Kruger Bobs replied. "Syb no tell." "But why not?"

The matter-of-course question appeared to fill Kruger Bobs with amazement.

"Boss make night march," he answered. "She may not care to have me. Still, we'll ride out there with you in the morning."

"Boss?"

"Mr. Carew and myself."

Kruger Bobs looked hurt. In hot excitement, the black fingers closed on a fold of the brown sleeve.

"Kruger Bobs go, too?"

"What makes you want to go?"

"Syb dere, Boss."

"I don't see what difference that makes," Weldon said reflectively.

Once more Kruger Bobs turned coy.

"Boss go see his vrouw; me go see Syb," he explained briefly.

Weldon's laugh astonished him; still more Weldon's answer.

"Oh, Kruger Bobs, you love-struck calf! Because you're in love with Syb, do you think it follows that I am in love with Miss Mellen?"

Kruger Bobs plotted geometrical problems with his left toe.

"Syb say," he replied at length. Then he raised his eyes from his problem. "Boss vrouw good," he ventured persuasively.

Weldon laughed again.

"So we all think. Mr. Carew knows her much better than I do, though, and Miss Mellen would be hurt, if he didn't go out to see her."

But Kruger Bobs stood his ground. "Boss Weldon go see his vrouw; Kruger Bobs go see his vrouw; Boss Carew no vrouw."

However, in spite of the advice of Kruger Bobs, Carew was at Weldon's side, as they rode through Winburg, the next morning.

Already the country was taking on the look of summer, and the dusty stretches of veldt were tinged here and there with thin patches of growing green. Over the hills nearest the town were scattered the lines of ruined trenches, still littered here and there with rusty tools dropped there by the Boers when, long months before, they had caught sight of the advancing armies of French and Hutton. As they drew nearer, Weldon could make out the familiar details of a field hospital: the low white tents in their circle of whitewashed stones, the Red-Cross nurses hurrying to and fro and the blue-coated convalescents strolling leisurely about the enclosure. Carew, meanwhile, had pushed forward. Above the P. M. O.'s tent fluttered the Red Cross, and he had caught sight of a white apron and a scarlet cape in the open door.

"Miss Mellen! Alice!"

In the still air of a summer noon, Carew's voice carried distinctly back to Weldon. He glanced towards the tent. Then, beckoning to Kruger Bobs, he turned and rode away to inspect the distant landscape.

An hour later, Kruger Bobs was squatting on the ground, a heaped plate on his knees and a smile of rapture surrounding his smacking lips. Near him, the three horses munched contentedly, stamping lightly now and then and whisking their tails to drive off the buzzing flies. Outside the door of the tent, Alice Mellen sat on a bench, with Carew at her side and Weldon sprawling lazily on the ground at her feet.

"Twenty-seven inside," she told them. "It is mostly enteric and S. C., men who have been sent here from Bloemfontein. Their hospitals are overcrowded. We have both sorts here, you know."

"Nursing Boers?" Carew asked, disapprovingly.

"Why not? They are men, plucky men, too, some of them. I rather like the race. Anyway, it makes an interesting mixture. We have had to put them all together, and they get on capitally, exchanging stories and gossip and sympathy like men of the same company. One of them, a Boer,--" she hesitated for the right word; then she adopted the vernacular of the service--"went out, the other day; and, among his mourners, the sincerest ones were the two London Tommies in the two next beds. War isn't all hatred, by any means. Turn nurse for a month and you'll find it out."

"Or else turn patient," Carew interpolated quietly.

Her color came; but she only turned more directly to Weldon.

"I was glad to come here for a change," she added. "Shall you stay here long?"

"It is impossible to tell. The other nurses here are younger at it than I, and there are some hard cases. If it were not for Syb, I should be at my wits' end sometimes."

"Then ought you to stay here?" Carew urged, with a sudden assumption of proprietorship which sat well upon him.

She faced him with a smile.

"Oh, but this is nothing in comparison with Johannesburg. There the work is agonizing. Between wounds and enteric, the place is crammed, and we can't get the nurses we absolutely need. My mother thought I was growing too tired, and she sent Syb up here to take care of me. Instead, I have pressed her into the service and trained her until she is one of the best nurses I have ever had under me. The men adore her, she is so strong and so full of her queer, jolly fun."

With his head pillowed on his arms, Weldon lay watching her thoughtfully. Under her piles of inky hair, her face looked thin, and the shadows lay heavy around her eyes. Nevertheless, the eyes were shining and the curves of the lips were all upward. Plainly the day had brought her a tonic; yet the past six months had told upon the girl pitilessly.

"But, for God's sake, when is it all to end?" he burst out suddenly.

"Tired of the service, Mr. Weldon?" she asked gravely, but with no accent of reproach.

"Not tired of my own. But the worst of it all comes back on you women, and that is maddening."

She smiled down at him, and the light in her eyes deepened and grew yet more womanly.

"It is all we can do to help, Mr. Weldon. Let us take what share we can. The work is hard, hard and discouraging; but--" involuntarily she glanced at Carew's happy, handsome face; "but now and then it brings its own reward."

The short silence was broken only by Kruger Bobs, scraping his spoon along his fast-emptying plate. Then Alice spoke again.

"You hear often from Cooee, Mr. Weldon?"

"Now and then. Not often."

"Did you know that she may come to us, after Christmas?"

"No," he said alertly. "To Johannesburg?"

She nodded.

"We need her, and my aunt has almost given her consent. The need grows greater, every day; we can't hold out much longer, unless we can have more help. Cooee isn't trained at all; but she has endless tact and she knows how to take orders. Unless January brings us fewer patients, I think she will come north for a month." "Does she wish to?"

Alice laughed.

"As a matter of mere conscience. Cooee hates lint and disinfectants and the hush of things; but she begins to see the need before her. She makes all manner of fun of me, and of the whole hospital scheme of things; but still I think she will come. My aunt opposes it; but we are trying to compromise on a month. That won't wear Cooee out, and the novelty will last for that length of time, and help keep up her enthusiasm."

"Did you know Captain Frazer is coming up, in a week or two?"

For an instant, Alice's eyes clouded.

"No. When did you hear?"

"Just as I left camp. The appointment took him quite by surprise, and he wrote to me at once," Weldon answered with quiet dignity, for he was not slow to read the question in the girl's mind.

Her face cleared.

"I hadn't heard. Cooee's last letter is three weeks old, so it couldn't bring the news." Then she glanced over her shoulder, as one of the doctors halted on the threshold. "Am I needed?"

"Young Walpole is just going," he said gravely. "He has asked for you."

Both men rose to their feet. It was Carew, however, who lingered.

"We are leaving Winburg, to-morrow, so this is good by," he said regretfully. "Take care of yourself, Alice, and bless you!" And, underneath its happiness, his boyish face was unusually grave, as he mounted and rode away at Weldon's side.

CHAPTER SEVENTEEN

Christmas morning found the camp at Lindley wakening to a general atmosphere of peace and good will to man. Scarcely fifty miles away at Tweefontein, De Wet's midnight charge had left behind it sixty men sleeping their last grim sleep in defiance of the peace ordained for the Christmas dawn. And, midway between the camp of the living and the line of the dead, there lay the little town of Bethlehem.

After the frosty night, the day came, hot and clear, with the sun beating down from a cloudless sky and the mirage dancing upon the distant horizon. To the men from the north, it was a bit of a shock to exchange Christmas greetings, while the thermometer went sliding up to the mark of one hundred degrees. Nevertheless, they hailed one another lustily, and threw themselves into the spirit of the holiday feast with the zest of schoolboys.

For full three months now, the greater number of the troopers had been dodging up and down over the surface of the Orange River Colony on the heels of the tireless De Wet. After accomplishing forty futile miles a day, after subsisting chiefly upon army biscuits and bully beef, they had earned their right to rest. This, at least, was the opinion of their adjutant.

All the day before, there had been flying rumors of a forced march on the following morning; but no orders had been given, and just at nightfall had come the definite announcement that no move would be made until after Christmas. Those who had seen their adjutant going away from the colonel's tent, half an hour before, were able to draw their own conclusions. The rest accepted the fact as it stood, and made no effort to account for the change in their plans. It was enough for them that two thousand sheep were to be roasted, to the end that every man might eat his fill; and they took an eager hand, next morning, in scooping out the ant-hill and kindling the fires inside. Then, seated on the ground, they spun their yarns while they waited until the white-hot earth on top of the hill gave notice that the oven was ready for the roast.

Carew, meanwhile, was unpacking the neat little parcel which had come to him with Christmas greeting from the Daughters of the Empire. Lined up for inspection before breakfast, every trooper had received an exactly similar parcel; every one had given expression to his thankful heart; then every one had gone away to inspect the offering.

"This is kind of the ladies, very kind," Carew was observing, with a perfectly grave face, as he drew out a handkerchief of spotty red cotton and a khaki-colored nightcap. "Look, Weldon! These fit my complexion to a charm, and will be wonderfully warm and comfortable. What is in your grab bag?"

"Ditto, apparently," Weldon answered. "I think I shall keep these to sport about at home in."

Carew shook his head.

"Oh, no. The kind ladies wish us to use them now, and you should accept the gift according to the spirit in which it is given." Taking off his wide felt hat, he replaced it with the wool nightcap, covered the nightcap with the handkerchief and then put on the hat over all the rest. "And what have we here?" he continued. "A pipe? Oh, the naughty ladies! Cigarettes?" He smelled at them gingerly, then sneezed into a corner of the scarlet kerchief. "Matches, shoelaces, and, by George, a cake of soap! Now, if we only had a farmer's almanac and a flannel chest-protector, we'd be quite complete."

Weldon laughed. Then he beckoned to a little trooper standing beside the nearest ant-hill.

"Paddy," he said gravely; "these toys are excellent toys. If anything should happen to me, I'll will them to you."

Paddy thrust his hand into his pocket, drew out his own nightcap and dangled it by its khaki-colored tip.

"And look at it!" he said slowly. "The spirit is willing and full of peace; but what would I be doing with that thing, I who never had a hat on my head till I was ten years old, let alone a cap?"

"Wrap your feet in it, then," Carew suggested. "It's large enough for them both. Paddy, who eats at your ant-hill?"

The little Irishman winked knowingly.

"Them as invites theirselves, first off. If it's you and Mr. Weldon, so much the better for Paddy. The rum ration is doubled, the day; knowing the habits of you both, I'm thinking I see my way to getting six times gloriously drunk. There's beer by the hogshead, too. It'll be a mighty Christmas dinner, the first in years I've eaten without cooking."

"You generally eat it raw?" Carew questioned blandly.

"Praised be Patrick, no; but it's Paddy who has done the cooking. This year, I am free from my pots and kettles, and can eat with the best of them. Little

Canuck dear, don't ever enlist as a cook. Nothing spoils the stomach of you like the smell of the warming broth."

"You like the change, then, Paddy?" Weldon asked, as he thriftily packed up his parcel and stowed it away in his pocket, with an eye to the gratitude of Kruger Bobs.

"Like, is it? I rejoice greatly and shout, as the Book bids us. It's a man's work I'm doing now; it's with men that I am doing that work, and it's a man who leads me on to do that work, meaning Captain Frazer."

"Where is the Captain now?"

Paddy dropped down on the ground, midway between his friends and his ant-hill.

"Over yonder, doing the work of an honest man and a warrior."

"That goes without saying. What now?"

But Paddy chose to speak in metaphors.

"He's thrown down his sword and picked up his bottle," he responded enigmatically.

"Not drinking?" Weldon asked incredulously.

"No, little one; not doing, but doing by. He's administering advice and physic to them cormyrants of Queenslanders. The Colonials are a hard race to manage and a greedy." Paddy spoke with an accent of extreme disfavor.

"What have the poor Queenslanders done?"

"Poor it is; not poor in spirit, but poor in judgment. They've converted the top course of their dinner into the bottom course of their breakfast, and now they're suffering according. Next time, when their kyind officers order them up, each a little Crosse and Blackwell plum pudding, they'll know enough to eat them up hot on a full stomach, not bolt them down cold on top of a lone layer of dog-bread. Man is permitted to make such errors but once in his life, without having Providence get after him and slay him. Little Canuck?" "Paddy?"

"The top of the ant-hill is white with heat, and the lambie must enter the roasting tomb. Will you and Mr. Carew eat with me?"

"We've no intention of eating anywhere else, Paddy. We know your cooking of old."

"It's an honor you'll be doing me, then. And, moreover--" Paddy hesitated, with the words sticking to his lips.

"What now?"

"Think you the Captain--I mean the Adjutant; but he'll always be the Captain to me--would he take it amiss, think you, little one, if I sent him a bit of the joint, for the sake of old times? He'll like be eating truffled ostrich and locust sauce at the mess; but Paddy'd like to have a hand in his Christmas dinner. It's all I can do for him, and he's done much for me."

"Try him and see, Paddy," Weldon advised. "If I know Captain Frazer, he'll have nothing to-day that will please him more."

With feasting and story-telling and the inevitable letters to wife and sweetheart, the sunshiny day lost itself in twilight and the twilight in the chill of night. Along the line of the blockhouses for miles away, lights began to twinkle out from the narrow loopholes. Throughout the camp, answering lights twinkled back at them till the night was spotted thick with dots of yellow, winking up at the yellow stars above. And around the camp and the blockhouses lay the dark, measureless veldt, and the veldt was very still.

Stillness was not in the camp, however. Even the gluttonous Queenslanders had recovered from their woes of the morning; and, from end to end of the great enclosure, there was a spirit of merrymaking born of the feast day, the dinner and the unwonted allowance of rum. In the groups scattered about the camp fires, tongues wagged freely of home, of boyhood, of adventures in past years. War talk was tabooed that night. According to his custom, Tommy ignored the present and ranged at large over the remote past and yet remoter future.

Carew, with the easy adaptability which marked him, was the central figure of one of the groups where he acted as a species of toastmaster, to direct the trend of the stories and lead the singing. Weldon sat slightly apart, watching the firelit group before him, while his mind trailed lazily to and fro, from home, with its holly wreaths in the windows, to Cape Town where the flower-boxes edging a wide veranda would be a mass of geranium blossoms now, and where, in the shady western end, would sit a tall girl with hair the color of the yellow flame. Strangely enough, to his honest, straightforward mind it never occurred to doubt that she was thinking of him, sending a Christmas wish in his direction. More than once she had given proof of her liking for him, her interest in his concerns. Her blue eyes had met his eyes steadily, kindly. Weldon had certain old-fashioned notions of womanhood which not all of his social life had been able to beat out of him. Far back in his boyhood, his mother, still a social leader at home, had told him it was unmanly to flirt. A good and loyal woman would have no share in flirtation; women of the other sort could have no share in his life. Weldon was no Galahad. He had danced and dined with many women, had given sympathy to some, chaff to others; nevertheless, his relations with them had been curiously direct and simple. Quite unconsciously to himself, his mother's code had become ingrained in the very fibre of his being. And now he was ready to stand or fall by his judgment that Ethel Dent, Cooee as he called her in his secret heart, was as good and loyal as a woman could be. The future seemed to him so obvious that he made no effort to forecast it. He was content to wait.

"Christmas is nearly over, Weldon."

He roused himself abruptly, as Captain Frazer dropped down at his side.

"Yes; but the revel will outlast the day," he answered, laughing. "Tommy is in his glory now, and it will take more than taps to make him subside."

"Perhaps. He has rioted most joyously. Christmas has been no empty mockery to him." Weldon's quick ear detected a ring of melancholy in the Captain's voice.

"Has it to you?"

The Captain sat silent for a moment, his eyes fixed on the winking fires.

"Not really. Of course, we all have been a bit homesick, and I can see no shame in confessing it. Besides, after one gets out of his windsor-tie stage of life, these especial holidays seem to mark time so. One thinks back to this time, last year; and one has to wonder a bit where he will be, a year from now. A good deal can happen in a year."

"For better, or for worse," Weldon added.

The words caught the Captain's ear.

"Yes, for better or for worse," he repeated; "in sickness and in health. A year is a long time. Tell me, have you heard lately from Miss Dent?"

Long afterwards, the question came back to Weldon, with the obvious association of ideas. Now he answered, with perfect unconcern,--

"Not for three or four weeks."

"I have heard since you, then. She wrote, last week, and sent greeting to you and Mr. Carew."

"Thank you. Give mine back to her; that is, if you are writing."

"I shall write, to-night," the Captain said briefly.

"Then please send her my wishes for Christmas and New Year's both. You might also remind her to write to me. She writes wonderfully good letters." Turning his eyes from the fire, the Captain watched him steadily for a moment. Unconscious of his companion's gaze, Weldon was staring out across the camp, his lips framed to a noiseless whistling, his face full of dreamy content. The Captain studied the happy, resolute young face, drew a deep breath and then turned to the fire once more.

"Yes," he assented. "But you would know that, from hearing her talk."

Suddenly, Weldon's lips straightened, and he faced the Captain directly.

"I like Miss Dent," he said frankly. "Of course, you know that. But, moreover, I have always felt I owed her a debt of gratitude for introducing me to you. I know one doesn't usually say such things, Captain Frazer," he laughed, in sudden boyish embarrassment; "but it is a little different on Christmas night, you know. Next year, we may be miles apart, and so, if you don't mind, I'd like to say that you have been wonderfully good to me, this year, and that I appreciate it."

Captain Frazer took the outstretched hand, slim, but hard now, and a bit stubby about the nails.

"Thank you, Weldon," he answered. "This may be our only Christmas together, and I am glad you told me."

The silence about them was broken by the voices of the soldiers singing around the camp fires and by the bagpipes playing somewhere across the distance. Then, after a little, they fell to talking of other things, with the natural antipathy of healthy men to any recurrence of a momentary outburst of sentiment.

Around them, the fires flared and flamed across the darkness; beyond them, the veldt stretched away, sinister, mysterious; and from above the stars twinkled down upon them, smiling a Christmas blessing alike on those who were doomed to glory and those who were doomed to death. For an instant, the sudden pause in the singing and laughter seemed typical of the short, sudden pause in their active lives. Then, as the Captain rose, the singing broke out once more, Carew's voice leading.

"Good-night, Weldon. I must go back to my quarters."

"And to your letters?"

"Yes, to my letters. And may next Christmas be good to us both!"

Weldon rose and saluted, then stood looking after his companion as he walked away, head and shoulders erect and his lips smiling slightly, as if in anticipation of the task before him. And, meanwhile, from the fire near by came the lusty chorus,--

"A little brown cot, a shady green spot, No happier home I find. My heart's fairly gone, for I love only one, She's the gi-irl I le-eft behind."

The voices, rollicking even in their sentimentality, dropped away into silence; the fire flared up and then suddenly died away into darkness. But, even in the darkness, Weldon could see the dim outline of the Captain's figure, moving steadily forward along his self-appointed way.

CHAPTER EIGHTEEN

Lord Kitchener, one night in early February, was sitting on the apex of a vast triangle in the northern end of the Orange River Colony. Two sides of the triangle were made up of long lines of blockhouses, strung on a chain of barbed-wire fencing. The blockhouses were of loop-holed stone or iron with iron roofs, and they were separated from each other by only a few hundred yards. The barbed-wire chain which strung together these zigzag lines was five strands wide, and it was edged with a five-foot trench and now and then with an additional length of stone wall. Beyond the fences were the railroad lines, and up and down over the tracks armored trains carrying search-lights were running to and fro, to shed all possible light upon the fences and upon the enclosure beyond. The third side of the triangle consisted of an infinite number of men in khaki, and its density varied entirely according to its position. At first, it opened out to a thin line of troopers scattered over the arc of an immense circle; then it drew in until an army stood in fighting array straight across the veldt from Heilbron to Kroonstad. And Wolvehoek was the apex of the triangle.

Experience had taught the master brain of the British army that it was useless longer to chase De Wet up and down over the face of the earth. The Boer general was familiar with every crack and cranny of that earth. He knew where to hide, where to dodge, where to scurry away as fast as his convoy train could bear him company. Behind him, plucky, but totally in ignorance of the natural advantages of the country, toiled and perspired and skirmished the British army. Horses were exhausted, men were killed and supply wagons were captured, all to little or no purpose. If the quarry could not be taken by direct pursuit, it was needful to have recourse to the methods of the ranch. Pursuit failing, it was time for a round-up.

To this end, the Orange River Colony had been marked off into sections by the rows of blockhouses strung upon barbed wire. Drive after drive had been made into these enclosures; and every drive had brought its bag of game. But still the general himself had eluded them. Early in February, however, a giant drive had been planned, directed away from the enclosure in order that, once De Wet took refuge in his usual trick of doubling back upon his pursuers, he should find himself caught in the open trap. And, secure in the ultimate success of his plan, Lord Kitchener waited at Wolvehoek in expectation of its end.

The drive had been made, De Wet had doubled, and now the base of the triangle was flowing in upon him, fully confident of success at last. And the base was in part made up of the South African Light Horse, and Carew and Weldon were of that Horse, and they rejoiced accordingly.

Nightfall of the sixth found the quarry well inside the triangle, and the South

African Light Horse drawn up in a straight line running westward from Lindley. The officers slept in their boots, that night, and every trooper held himself tense in his blankets, ready to cease snoring at an instant's notice. And far away to the northward, the moving search-lights carved the frosty darkness with their blinding cones of light.

Weldon was ordered out on picket duty, that night. All day long, he had ridden hard, until even the zeal of Piggie had begun to flag. Nevertheless, as the broad stripe of yellow reluctantly died out of the western sky, his excited brain denied to his tired muscles the sleep which they demanded. Accordingly, it was a relief when his orders came, and he found himself advancing cautiously out into the shadowy veldt.

Contrary to his usual mood when on picket, Weldon had no sense of loneliness, that night. Reaching away from him on either hand was the huge enclosing wall of humanity, pacing to and fro on picket duty, guarding the blockhouses, patrolling the wire fences between. Every man was alert to his duty; every nerve was taut with the consciousness that somewhere within the cordon was the leader who heretofore had escaped them, that each man was a link forged in the endless chain which was stretched around the invisible enemy. And, meanwhile, the starless sky and the waiting chain were equally silent and equally freighted with mystery. And the future seemed full of portent and very near.

Then, as the midnight hour swung past him, Weldon heard the rustle of a quiet footfall. It was Captain Frazer's voice that answered his challenge.

"I was looking for you, Weldon," he added.

"For anything especial?"

"No. I felt restless and couldn't sleep, so I thought I would go the round of the pickets. They said you were out here. Where is Carew?"

"In my sleeping-bag. I don't encourage him for a neighbor just now. He draws too much fire."

The Captain laughed softly.

"He is an unlucky beggar. Eight, nine, how many times is it that he has been hit? He ought to engage a private nurse."

"He has." And Weldon explained the little scene at the door of the hospital tent.

"Happy fellow! He deserves her, though. But it is an ideal combination, that of nurse and soldier," the Captain answered lightly. Then he asked, "What sort of a day have you had?"

"Rousing. Now the question is: what sort of a night are we going to have?"

"The night of our lives, I suspect," the Captain replied, still in the low tone in which all their talk had been made. "The orders are to close in at daylight, and work the game up towards Wolvehoek; but, if I know anything at all of De Wet, he won't wait till daylight."

"You think he will fight?"

"If he does, it will be a fight to the finish," the Captain said gravely.

Weldon's grip tightened on his rifle.

"When will it come?"

"Heaven only knows. Probably just before light. He will take this end of things, on account of avoiding the railroads and--"

Weldon's hand shut on his arm.

"Hush! What's that?"

Swiftly the Captain's gravity vanished, and he laughed.

"By George, here they are!" he exclaimed.

From the veldt to the northward, there came a confused din of rushing, trampling feet; a cloud of dust, lifted on the night breeze, swept down upon them; and then a herd of stampeding cattle dashed madly past, noses to earth and tails lashing in furious fear. An instant later, the darkness to the left was shattered by dots of light, and the air snapped with the double crack of Mauser rifles. Far to the northward, though muffled by distance, there was more firing, and yet more; and ever the moving searchlights carved their way to and fro through the inky night.

Like a dog on the scent and ready for the plunge, Captain Frazer had straightened to the full of his height and stood tense, waiting an instant to measure the scope of the coming fight.

"It's a row, sure enough; and thank God, I'm in it!" he said quietly then. "Come back to the line, Weldon. There'll be work for us all, in a few minutes."

Even as he spoke, and while they were hurrying back to the squadron, a random shot pierced the darkness just before them, and a bullet whirred close above their heads. Another shot tossed up a spray of dust at their feet, and a third fell full in the tent where Carew was swiftly tightening his belts and assuring himself that his bandoliers were full.

They found the camp already humming like a hive of angry bees. A small matter of forty miles a day counted for nothing to men wakened from heavy sleep to face the firing of an invisible foe. There was no need of the murmured report that De Wet had bidden his followers break through the British chain wherever its links were weakest. Instinctively each man threw himself into fighting array, convinced that the present minute marked the climax of the past days.

And, meanwhile, the limitless darkness shut down over the determined cordon of British men facing steadily inward towards the foe which they could not see; over the scattered knots of Boer horsemen, secure in their full knowledge of every yard of the ground, riding forward to fight their way through the chain into the veldt beyond. And, far to the northward, De Wet was lurking in shadow long enough to cut the wires and then ride away with his trio of faithful followers.

To Weldon, fresh from the darkness and silence of the open veldt, it seemed as if, of a sudden, the frosty night were tattered into shreds. As the fight waxed hot about him, he lost all memory of the intermediate stages. At one instant, all had been still and dim; at another, the air before him was thick with vivid rifle flashes, his ears were full of the strident din of flying bullets, of shouting men, of squealing, moaning horses. For a time, he could see nothing of the enemy but the flashing dots of fire. Then the dots drew nearer, closed up, and the din was increased by the rattle of fixing bayonets, by the dull, sucking sound of steel prodded into soft masses, and by the thud of falling bodies. And always from the outer circle the pitiless rain of bullets came splashing down upon them, striking impartially on friend and on foe.

Side by side in the foremost rank, Weldon and Carew were fighting like tigers. Carew's cheek was gashed by a passing bullet, and Weldon's coat showed dark and wet over his left shoulder; but neither man was conscious of pain, or of fear, or of anything else than a surly determination to check the maddening rush before them. Carew was slashing about him with all the strength of arm and bayonet; but Weldon, disdaining his bayonet, was firing with a steady aim which sent one man and then another to join the heap on the ground at his feet.

A second bullet grazed his wrist, and a horseman swept down upon him. For an instant, he wavered. Then he straightened his shoulders and took careful aim. From ten feet away, he had heard a ringing order, and the order had been given, not in the voice of his own captain, but in that of Captain Frazer who, as ranking officer, had taken command of the fight into which chance had led him. Weldon's every nerve answered to the tonic of that voice. Not since Vlaakfontein had he been under its command. Nevertheless, the old spell was upon him, and he responded to its call. An instant before, the rush towards him had seemed indomitable. Those furious, fighting horsemen could not be stayed in their course. Now he braced himself for the shock of their coming, while tired hand and blurring eye roused themselves to do the bidding of his brain. He was dimly aware that Paddy had struggled forward to his other side and, shoulder to shoulder with him, was helping to beat back the iron-like force pressing down upon them. Then, with the keen grasp of trifling detail which often marks the supreme moment of mental exhaustion, he became conscious that the hairy tail which brushed across his face was unduly coarse and tangled, while a sudden cheer from around him told that the Boers were turning in flight.

Dazed, he drew his hand across his face, and stared wonderingly at the scarlet drops on his fingers. Then he turned and looked down at Paddy with a whimsical, questioning smile. Paddy repeated his query.

"Are you hurt, little one?" he demanded, for the second time, as he shook Weldon's arm.

Weldon steadied at the touch.

"No; only scratched a bit. It is nothing to last at all. Are you all right?"

Paddy shut his hand over a shattered finger.

"Glory be! And the snakes of Boers is wriggling off to their holes. And now, where's the Captain?"

They found him a little apart from the line, slightly to the front and close beside a scattered heap of bearded men. His face was white and the lines of his face were rigid and drawn; but he hailed them just as he always had been used to do.

"My luck has changed," he added quietly. "They have taken my leg, this time. Still, it's not so very painful. I'll fill my pipe first, and then will you two fellows help me back, till we can find an ambulance?"

CHAPTER NINETEEN

In a quiet corner of the crowded hospital at Johannesburg, one narrow bed was screened away from its neighbors. Beside the bed sat Ethel Dent, and Weldon leaned against the wall beyond. Both of them were smiling bravely down into the dark-fringed blue eyes which met their eyes with a steady wishfulness. With the end so plain in sight, why keep up the pretence of being blind to its approach?

An operation had been the final chance, and the chance had failed. Out from the stupor of ether, out from the hours of bewildering pain, Captain Frazer had come back to an interval of full consciousness, of fuller knowledge that, for him, this painless interval was but the prelude to the final painless sleep. Nevertheless, the man who had helped other men to die unflinchingly was facing death with a grave, unflinching smile, albeit life to him was good and full of promise. The interval was short. He would pass through it in manlike fashion, and, meanwhile, give thanks that beside his bed sat the one woman in whom his whole future so long had centered.

The slow moments passed by, unheeded. It was an hour since the surgeons had gone away; it was nearly an hour since Alice Mellen had followed the surgeons. Instinctively she realized that her place was otherwhere. There was no need now for skilled nurses. Ethel could do all the little which would be required, and it was Ethel's right to stay.

Since Alice had left them, no word had been spoken. The Captain had little strength for words as yet. It was taking all his energy and courage to face the truth and to accept it. Only an hour before, his crippled career had seemed to him unbearable. Now, as he lay with his eyes fixed on the girl beside him, he realized how much of potential sweetness that dreary alternative had held. And yet, Fate had drawn him into the battle, and it was something that he had met Fate bravely and in the foremost rank. So far, he had never funked a fight; if it took his last bit of strength, he would go pluckily through this last, worse fight which he was destined to face. He stirred slightly, and shut his teeth on his lower lip; but his eyes never dropped from Ethel's face. From the farther side of the bed, Weldon, too, was watching Ethel. If he lived to full fivescore years, he could never forget her face as he had met her at the hospital door, that morning. Exhausted with the excitement of the battle, stiff with his half-dressed wounds, soiled and untidy and haggard, he had paused beside the ambulance while the attendants had lifted the stretcher and borne the Captain up the low flight of steps. Then, like a man in a dream, he had followed along behind them until, on the very threshold, he had raised his heavy eyes to see Ethel standing before him, a broad shaft of sunshine pouring down upon her to rest in the locks of sunshiny hair which straggled out from beneath her crisp white cap.

"Cooee!" he said huskily, as he took her hand. Then, for the first time in all those terrible hours since the battle, his lips had quivered, and two big, boyish tears had rolled out across his cheeks.

Already the fight seemed to him to be months old. From the first, it had been the Captain's wish that Weldon should go with him to the hospital, and Weldon would have allowed no other man to go in his place. Wounded and weak from loss of blood, nevertheless he forgot his own weakness as he saw the leg, shattered by two bullets, explosive bullets such as are denied to warfare of any but barbarous nations. Young though he was, Weldon had seen many a man wounded before now. He was not slow to realize the nature of the alternatives which lay before the man who was at once his hero and his friend. Mercifully, he had as yet no knowledge how soon the one alternative must be taken from him.

The case was too grave a one for the surgeons of the field hospital. In after years, that ambulance journey into Kroonstad seemed branded upon Weldon's memory: the baking heat of the February sun, the interminable miles of dusty road stretching away between other interminable miles of grassy veldt, scarred and seamed here and there with ridges of naked rock. And at last the ambulance had jogged into Kroonstad, only to find that no help lay in the hospital there, that the journey must be dragged onward through a night ride to Johannesburg.

If the jolting, crawling ambulance had been bad, the jarring train was infinitely worse. The Captain made no complaints; he was grateful for every slight attention; he even forced himself to joke a little now and then. Nevertheless, Weldon, sitting beside him and occasionally laying his own fingers across the steady hand on the blanket, was maddened by the noise of the engine, by the ceaseless thud, thud as the wheels took every new rail, by the roar, and the rush, and the dust which filtered in upon them. There was nothing he could do. He merely sat there beside his friend, and thought. Occasionally, he thought of Ethel; but, for the most part, his mind was on the man before him, the man whose active career all at once had been cut in two. Now and then he thought of the one who had chosen to fire those bullets, taboo of all but the most brutal warfare. At such times, he rose and fell to pacing restlessly up and down the car. Then he controlled himself and resumed his seat.

Moment by moment, almost second by second, the dreary night had worn away. It was full morning when the train had halted inside the familiar station. After his vigil, the healthy stir of the streets appeared to Weldon like the confused picture of a dream, and it had been like a man in a dream that he had been driven away to the hospital. Then, on the steps, he had seen Ethel, and the dream had been shattered, giving way, for the instant, to the perfect happiness of reality.

But the surgeons at Johannesburg had shaken their heads. The delay, although unavoidable, had been full of danger. One only chance remained, and they would take that chance. Weldon had lingered until he was ordered away; then, with Ethel beside him, he had gone to find a doctor who could dress his own wounds and make him fit to face the ordeal which he knew was awaiting him. For one short moment, he had felt Ethel's hands busy about his shoulder and head and wrist, had rejoiced in the quiet strength of their soothing touch. For another moment, their eyes had met; but no word had been spoken between them. Then Alice had come to them, bringing the surgeon's verdict. That had been an hour before. Now they still were there, watching the slow approach of the inevitable summons.

Slowly the day waxed--and waned. For the waning life, there was no interval of waxing. Slowly, steadily, by infinitesimal degrees, Leo Frazer was sinking down into the Valley of the Shadow. Once the head surgeon had stepped behind the screens and bent over the bed. Only Ethel had seen the brief contraction of his brows; but no one of them was deceived by his cheery words of parting. And still the blue eyes rested upon Ethel, as if seeking to gain from her the answer to some unspoken question, as if begging her to share with him some fraction of her quiet strength. Now and then Ethel wondered at her own quiet. This was the second week of her promised month with her cousin; but it was the first time she had come face to face with death, the first time, too, that her work had taken on any hint of personality. Now, suddenly confronted with these three, Death and the two men who, during the past fourteen months, had played so active parts in her life, she was surprised to find that she faced them steadily and in silence. As yet, she felt no wish to make any moan. That would come later, when her nerves had relaxed a little from the stretching strain. And, meanwhile, as she sat watching the face on the pillow, grieving for the waning life, now and then she raised her eyes to the other face on the opposite side of the bed, and told herself that Fate, harsh as it was, was yet not altogether unpitying. Although wounded and worn and sick at heart, Weldon was with her, and intensely alive.

"Ethel!"

Bending forward, she laid her strong, firm hand upon the hand of the Captain, noting, as she did so, that the finger tips were cold to her own warm touch.

"Yes?" she said gently.

"You are here? It troubles me to see. Stay with me to the end, Ethel. It won't be so very long."

She bowed her head; but the answer came firmly.

"I will stay."

There was a short silence. Then, gathering together all his strength, the Captain went on quite steadily,--

"It won't be so very long, Ethel. I am sorry. I liked to live. I have had a good time, and I had no idea that my good times were so nearly over. Not that it would have made much difference, though. And yet, when one comes to the end, all of a sudden, one finds a great many things that are left unfinished."

She made no attempt to answer.

Gently he urged the final words upon her attention.

"There are always so many things left unfinished," he repeated.

"Yes," she said faintly.

Slowly, as if its weight dragged sorely upon his failing strength, he raised her hand to the pillow and rested his cheek upon it.

"Don't cry, Ethel," he said then. "Of course, if I had lived, it might have meant so much to us both."

Involuntarily she caught her breath and made a swift gesture, as if to withdraw her hand. Then, with a hasty glance at Weldon, leaning against the opposite wall, she controlled herself and allowed her hand to rest where it was.

"It would have meant so much to all of us, Captain Frazer."

"Perhaps. But to you and me--Ethel, I can't go out of life and give you up!" Pitifully, longingly, the blue eyes stared up at her face through the growing shadows of waning day and waning life. Longingly, although the questioning look had left them. In its place was an infinite, contented love, an absolute trust.

The girl nerved herself to meet his eyes. Then she drew her own eyes away, to give another hasty, appealing glance up into Weldon's paling face. For him, as for her, the moment was all unexpected. For him, as for her, there was need of all the reserve strength in life to go through it honorably and without flinching.

Up to that very hour, no thought of Leo Frazer's love had crossed the mind of

Ethel Dent. They had been friends, good comrades, meeting often and always with much pleasure. She had acknowledged to herself, long since, that he was a man among men; she honored him, admired him, cared for him as she might have cared for an only brother. Beyond that, she could not go. Moreover, it had never occurred to her that Captain Frazer could mistake her attitude to himself, could differentiate her light, bright cordiality from the cordiality she showed to other men. When she had met him first, she had been a mere girl in character and experience; love had had scant place in her girlish dreams. Later, Weldon had come into her life. His coming had changed many things for her; but it had made no change in her attitude to the Captain. She was now, as always, his loyal, admiring friend, no less, no more. She had supposed that he had felt the same loyal friendship for her. Too late, she realized her mistake.

"You must have known it all, Ethel," the Captain was saying steadily; "how my whole life has seemed to go into yours. I have never told you. I was sure you knew it, without any telling, and I have been waiting until the war was over, before asking you to go home with me, as my wife. The--" he caught his breath sharply, "the war is over for me now, dearest. I can't ask you to go home with me; but--Tell me, Ethel, I have not been mistaken, all these months? You have cared for me, as I have cared for you?" The last words came out with the roundness of tone he had used in health; but there was a weary drag to the hand that drew her hand still nearer to his cheek. Ethel faltered. Then, soldier-like, she braced herself to fight to a finish. It was not her fault that the man had mistaken her friendly, cordial liking for something deeper, infinitely more lasting. She had never consciously played with him, never sought to win his love. Blame there was none; it was all only a mistake, albeit a terrible one. Nevertheless--

Desperately she glanced up from the blue eyes, still so wishfully fixed upon her own, up to the drawn, white face of the haggard man on the farther side of the bed. In that instant, the girl fought madly with herself. Then her eyes dropped back to the bed once more. Eternity and time; a final short, comforting word to the one, a long explanation to the other. The mistake, if mistake there were, had been all of her doing. Bravely she would take the bitter consequences. Captain Frazer's day was passing fast. The night remained for her talk with Weldon. Her eyes dropped back to the bed, and her hand yielded itself to the pressure of the ice-cold fingers.

"Yes," she said slowly and so faintly that Weldon, standing breathless, could scarcely hear the words; "I have cared for you, as you have cared for me."

The fingers tightened over her hand; but the lids drooped heavily above the dark blue eyes.

"Dearest--girl." Then, smiling to himself, Captain Leo Frazer fell asleep. The next moment counted itself out by slow seconds. Then Ethel raised her head and turned to smile drearily up at Weldon.

Instead, she found herself smiling up at an empty wall. Harvard Weldon had vanished and had left for her no word of farewell.

CHAPTER TWENTY

Up Commissioner Street and down Commissioner Street and around and around Market Square tramped a haggard man in khaki who surveyed all things with dull, unseeing eyes. On his cheek, an inch or so above his stubbly beard, was a wide cross of plaster, and his left wrist wore a narrow bandage. He walked with quick, nervous strides; yet every now and then he halted to rest for a moment. Then he hurried on again, as if pursued by some unseen, but malignant foe.

Twice he turned northward and paused before the hospital, staring irresolutely up at the lighted windows. Then, facing about abruptly, he moved on, swiftly, but with the mechanical tread of a man in a dream. Once he found himself resting on the steps of the Jewish synagogue. The next time he roused himself to take note of his surroundings, he was at the Berea Estate, following Hospital Hill straight to the eastward. It was then that he had turned about and faced back to the hospital. A scant half-dozen hours before, that hospital had held what was all the world to him. Now, without warning, that all had proved to be naught.

The blow had come crashing upon him, straight between the eyes and so suddenly that there had been no time for him to brace himself to meet it. From the moment of his facing Ethel in the doorway of the hospital, that noon, he had been sure that the talk which he would have with her, that evening, could bring but the one ending. At sight of the soiled and haggard man before her, her blue eyes had lighted with something far more than pleased surprise. His appearing had been quite unexpected; her meeting with him had been the naked impulse of her girlish heart. And, all that endless day, her grief for the Captain had in no way hidden her evident pleasure in his own presence. And then, all at once, had come the end, unexpected and hence doubly crushing. His young, newborn happiness was as little strong to bear the blow as were his exhausted body and his shattered nerve. Like a wild beast wounded to the death, he had crept silently away, to go through his agony, unseen.

Standing under the fierce glare of the electric light by the hospital gate, his appearance would wellnigh have baffled the recognition of his mother. Soiled and stained and tattered, his head sunk between his shoulders, he looked a feeble man of middle years. Dark shadows lay around his heavy gray eyes, and the corners of his mouth drooped pitifully. And, somewhere inside that building, was the girl who had snatched away from him what was dearer than life itself. For six long months she had been the incentive to all of his best work; it had been her influence which finally had led him to come back into the firing line; it had been in the hope for the future, a hope growing less and less vague as the months passed by, that he had been willing and glad to prolong his stay through one more torrid African summer. And to what end?

Strange to say, it never once occurred to him to try to win her love now, after all that bad passed. Still less did it occur to him to doubt the truth of her final words to the Captain. Weldon had missed the look of appealing anguish in the blue eyes which she had lifted to his; but he had heard the low, steady voice, had seen the pressure of the living fingers answer to the slight movement of the hand already growing cold. He had heard, and seen. It was enough. Always he had believed implicitly in Ethel's truth. There was no reason he should distrust her now. It was only that he had been an egregious ass to think that be could win her love, in the face of a man like Captain Leo Frazer. With a mighty effort, he straightened his shoulders, faced the wing where he knew the Captain would now be lying and reverently removed his hat. Then, for one last time, his eyes swept over the building and, turning away, he crawled off towards the railway station.

And, meanwhile, alone in a room behind one of those brightly-lighted windows, a girl sat huddled together, her crossed arms on her knees and her face buried in her arms, while she wailed to herself over and over again,--

"He might have waited! He might have waited! My God in heaven, what have I done? But at least he might have waited!"

A commissariat train was leaving Johannesburg at two o'clock the next morning. His pass in his hand, Weldon clambered drearily on the train for the long ride back to Kroonstad. Motion of any kind was better than remaining longer in Johannesburg. Nevertheless, the jolting of the train was wellnigh unbearable. His shoulder throbbed, and the dull pain in his head was maddening. He had passed the stage of weariness, however, where one is conscious of exhaustion. An ever-tightening strain was upon him. He could not rest now; he must go on, and on, and on, faster and ever faster, until at last something should snap and quiet perforce should overtake him.

Early dawn found him at Kroonstad. Sleep had been impossible for him; he had no appetite for food, and it took an ever-increasing effort for him to pull himself together. Like a man mounting a steep, pathless hill, he tried to drag himself up above the consciousness of his aching head and throbbing wounds; but it was not to be done. At the station he halted irresolutely. Then of a sudden he faced towards the great hospital tent.

"I want something to steady me a bit," he said briefly to the first doctor he met there. "I have two or three scratches, and I am feeling fagged. Give me something to help me get a grip on myself again, for I can't spend time to be ill."

The doctor remonstrated; but Weldon's answer was peremptory.

"I tell you, I can't stop. Give me something and let me go. I've work at Lindley that must be done, and a convoy leaves in an hour."

An hour later he was trudging over the veldt in the direction of Lindley. Lindley was forty miles away; the roads were dusty, and the sun of early February struck down upon him with the heat of a belated summer. Nevertheless, at Lindley was his squadron, and with his squadron would be work. Never in all his past life had Weldon known this imperative need for work. In it now, and in its accompanying excitement and in its inevitable risk, would lie his ultimate salvation. For him, the future held but one plain duty, and that duty was to forget.

The experienced eye of the doctor had told him that the gaunt trooper was a sick man; it had also told him that the trooper's determination would outweigh his sickness, at least for the present crisis. He made no effort to penetrate the cause of that determination. He merely yielded to it. A doctor less wise would have ordered Weldon into bed. This one saw further. He knew that a delicately adjusted machine often receives its worst damage from the friction needed to stop the whirring wheels. Better to wait and let them run down, untouched.

The forty miles from Kroonstad to Lindley were reducing themselves from a geographical fact to a matter of physical and mental anguish. There had been no rain for days, and under the burning sun, the dusty veldt seemed dancing up and down before Weldon's tired, feverish eyes. Now he passed through a stretch of bare and burned- out sand; now he tramped over patches of tall dry grass; now he plodded wearily around a heap of smooth black stones. Brick-red ant- hills higher than his knees dotted themselves over the veldt, their shell-like surface shielding a crowded insect colony within. Ant- bear holes lurked unseen in his pathway, tripping his heedless steps; and an occasional partridge went whirring upward, making him start aside in causeless terror at the unwonted sound. And over it all rested the glaring, shimmering, blinding light, laden with myriad particles of dazzling red-brown dust. Later still, the red-brown color vanished, and he walked for weary leagues over the fire-blackened veldt where the black rocks offered no contrast to the eye, and where the air was heavy with ashes caught up and scattered by the light breeze which heralded the coming night. And it was all so lonely, so hostile, so limitless. But no more lonely and hostile and limitless than the desolate future which stretched away and away before his gaze.

As yet he dared not trust his mind to rest too much upon the past. The future demanded his whole attention. It was a far cry for him from the present up to his limit of threescore years and ten. Still, he would not funk it now. That was the part of a sneak. Now, as always, he would stand by his young resolution to play out the game, to abide by the rules and to take the consequences. Nevertheless, it would be weary work to play out the game to its end, when the end held nothing for him in its keeping. His mind trailed off upon all sorts or vague corollaries scarcely connected with the fact. He recalled it with a jerk.

The Captain was dead. Ethel had loved the Captain. She had told the Captain of her love. As consequence, she could not love himself, Harvard Weldon. But he loved her. He had loved her for thirteen months and twenty-one days. Carefully he reckoned up the time; then, to make sure, he counted it off upon his fingers. Yes, he had loved her ever since that first lunch on the steamer, when she had snubbed him so roundly. He did not know it then. Looking backward, he knew it now. And there had been Cape Town, and Johannesburg, and Cape Town again. He stumbled into the open mouth of an ant-bear's hole and came down with a crash, full upon his wounded shoulder. Strange that his step should be so uncertain! Strange that he should feel so little inclination to swear! As he picked himself up, he wondered vaguely whether his pipe would be refreshing; but his wonder stopped, impotent to lead his dangling hand in the direction of his pocket. Then his mind took up its interrupted story, its record of brief, categorical facts.

He had meant to go home, that winter. Instead, Ethel had fanned the flame of his desire to go back to the front. He had left her, one evening, to pass a sleepless night, and, the next morning, to take himself out to enlist for another six months of service. The six months were nearly ended. Only three weeks remained. And then? Nothing.

The second night found him still far from Lindley. He had plodded on mechanically, stumbling often, but halting never, while his mind went whirling on and on, over and over the same old questions. His lips were feverish, and his eyes burned hotly, so it was almost with a sense of relief that he greeted the swift chill which followed the dropping of the sun. Over his head, the great arch of the sky shaded from east to west through every tint of purple and blue and turquoise and emerald-green, down to the golden band of the afterglow. Then the stars began to dot the purple, their tiny points of light serving only to emphasize its darkness, until the full moon swept up across the heavens, throwing its mystic silver light over all the land and adding tenfold to the empty loneliness of the veldt. Sleep was out of the question. He could only snuggle more closely into his blankets and wait for morning with what grace he could. The stopping of his physical action only increased the swiftness of his swirling thoughts which chased each other round and round in circling eddies about one fixed point. That point was Ethel.

Across the veldt at his left hand, he had watched the chain of blockhouses which lay along the country between Kroonstad and Lindley. Their squat outlines and the shining blue of their corrugated iron roofs had caught his wandering attention, held it, pinned it to other associations with those same blockhouses and, of a sudden, had brought him to a full realization that griefs did not come singly. He had left Johannesburg, to face a future apart from Ethel. He was coming back to Lindley, to face a future bereft of the Captain.

It was full noon, the next day, when the camp came into view. Leaving the convoy to follow in his wake, he headed straight for the rise where he had so often sat with Carew and gossiped of all things under the light of the sun. Then, as the round tents lay under his eyes like rows of dots punched into relief above the surface of the plain, he sank down on the coarse, parched grass and hid his eyes in his shaking hands. Yet even then the pitiless circle of tragic thoughts refused to stop their ceaseless round.

He roused himself at a touch on his arm. Kruger Bobs, at a distance, was eying him with a look of chastened welcome; but Carew stood beside him, one thin, sun-tanned hand on Weldon's shoulder.

"It's all right, old man," he was saying. "Don't try to tell me anything about it. Kruger Bobs saw you coming, and we rode out to meet you. Come in and rest. You look utterly done up."

Half way back to the camp, Carew spoke again; but it was only once.

"I told the fellows you were coming, and that you would be tired. They will keep out of your way, till you have had time to rest up a bit. Paddy is waiting to look out for you; but you needn't worry. He knows when to hold his tongue. If you need anything, or if you care to talk, send him out to look for me. Meanwhile, you need some rest."

CHAPTER TWENTY-ONE

"For God's sake, Weldon, how long is this going to last?"

Weldon raised his eyes from the seven-weeks-old Times in his hand, and looked at Carew in surprise.

"What last?" he questioned blankly.

Carew sprang to his feet and began to pace up and down with impatient, nervous steps.

"This. Everything," he said.

Weldon's smile, though it went no deeper than his lips, was half sarcastic, wholly sad.

"Specify," he advised languidly. "My mind can't grasp your generalities."

Carew took a few more turns. Then he came back to Weldon's side.

"It's this way, Harvey," he said slowly, for the moment lapsing into the name by which he had called his friend in their childhood; "since you came back from Johannesburg, you've not been the same man. What has done it?"

Weldon's lips shut with a tightness which curled the corners downward. Then, as he looked into the questioning eyes and anxious face of his companion, his own eyes softened, and he changed his mind in regard to keeping silence.

"It was a hard journey," he said evasively, yet with a kindly accent to the words. "Such days take it out of a man, Carew. I shall brace up in time."

Carew shook his head.

"That is just what you must not do. You have braced too long, as it is. Your wounds were nothing but scratches. They healed up easily enough, and you say, yourself, that they don't trouble you; but you look--"

"Well?" "As if things had ended for you," Carew blurted out desperately.

Slowly, wearily, Weldon lifted his eyes to his friend's face.

"Well, they have," he said, with an intonation of dreary finality.

"Rot!" Carew observed profanely. "Look here, Weldon, you've no business to funk in this fashion. It's not like you, either."

The word stung Weldon. He scrambled to his feet and stood to attention.

"Carew, no other man could say that to me," he said slowly.

Carew maintained his ground.

"No other man cares for you as I do, Harvey. We've been like brothers, and I have been too proud of your record to be willing to sit by, quiet, and see you spoil the last round of the game. There is too much at stake." Weldon raised his brows.

"What is at stake?" he asked coldly.

"Your whole army record. Your manhood. Your--" Carew hesitated; then he nerved himself to speak out plainly; "your love for Miss Dent."

Weldon shut his teeth and drew in his breath between them, while the dark red blood rushed across his face, and then died away, to leave in its place a grayish pallor. He put out his hand, as if to ward off something.

"For God's sake, don't!" he said huskily.

Carew watched him for an instant. Then he stepped forward and linked his arm through that of Weldon.

"There's nothing doing now," he said quietly. "Let's go for a walk. We can talk better, while we're moving, you know."

"But what is the use of talking?" Weldon objected listlessly.

Carew looked into the heavy eyes, the overcast face of his friend. Not once during the past three weeks since Weldon's return from Johannesburg had the cloud lifted.

"You must talk, Weldon," he said firmly. "If you don't talk, you'll go mad. I've watched you, day after day, hoping you would speak of your own free will. I have hated to urge you. It seemed rather beastly to drive you into telling me things that are none of my business. But they are my business, in a sense. There's nobody in all South Africa who can go back farther with you into the past. That alone ought to count for something."

Handsome still, in spite of his dark sunburn and his time-stained khaki, Carew's face was wonderfully attractive, as it looked into that of his friend. Weldon felt the attraction, even while he was wondering why it was so powerless to move him. He liked Carew; since the death of the Captain, no other man was linked more closely with his life. Nevertheless, Carew's words left him cold. All things did leave him cold of late. It was as if, in the fierce conflagration of that one hour in the Johannesburg hospital, the fires of his nature had burned themselves out beyond the possibility of being rekindled. His intellect told him that Carew was in the right of it, that his alternatives were speech or madness; but he faced the alternatives with an absolute indifference. His intellect also told him that, for the past three weeks, Carew's kindness had been unremitting; that his care had served as a buffer between himself and the clumsy tactlessness of their mates; that his sympathy now was leading him to try to storm the barrier of his own reserve; but he met Carew's advances with an icy front which could be thawed neither from outside nor from within. It was not his will to be ungrateful; it was beyond his present power to show the gratitude which he really felt. And Carew, with the supreme insight which marks the friendship of men at times, interpreted Weldon's mood aright and forebode to take offence.

Nevertheless, watching his friend closely, Carew had judged the case to be serious. He had felt no surprise at the state of collapse in which Weldon had struggled back into camp. The battle, the half- dressed wounds, the nerve-racking journey, the watching the slow approach of death and the accepting the fact of the loss of a valued friend: all these were enough to wreck the vitality of a man. With an almost womanish tenderness, Carew had brought his friend back to the tent, and made him over to the care of Paddy who gave up all things else, for the sake of his little Canuck. All that afternoon and night, Weldon lay passive, inert, while Paddy bathed him, fed him, poured cool, soft things over his wounds, fed him again, and then sat down beside him with his own stubby hand resting against Weldon's limp fingers. But, the next morning, Weldon rose, buttoned and belted himself with elaborate care. Then, disregarding the implorings of Carew and Paddy, who were terrified at the steady, unseeing look in his gray eyes and at the tense lines about his lips, he went to his captain and demanded his old position of regimental rough rider.

He obtained it. In fact, it was given, not only freely, but with joy. In all the regiment, no one else had been able to subdue such wild mounts as Weldon. In former days, he had stopped at little. Now he stopped at nothing. Horse-sickness, the scourge of South Africa, was in the land; and the underfed, overworked mounts yielded to it with pitiful ease. And, meanwhile, the need for horses was greater than ever. Drive after drive through the country about Kroonstad was bringing in the hostile Boers; but it was also bringing down the horses. The call for new mounts was limitless; limitless, too, the hours and the strength and the skill which Trooper Weldon put forth to the supplying that call. He was utterly untiring; but he was utterly reckless as well. Checked by no risk, sobered by no danger, he rushed into risk and danger as rushes the man whose one wish is to escape from a future of which he is in mortal, agonizing dread.

Carew said little; he watched much, and he meditated more. At first, he hoped all things from the healthy, outdoor life. He watched Weldon's muscles harden, saw his appetite return and welcomed with happy anticipations all the signs of his returning rugged strength. Then, as the time passed by, his anxiety came back upon him in full measure. Long days in the saddle were followed by sleepless nights; the shadow never came out of Weldon's eyes, the alertness never came back into his step. Lean, gaunt as a greyhound, he went about his work with a silent, dogged endurance which took no note of the other life about him. For Trooper Weldon, his profession had dropped to a dull, plodding routine of danger lapping close upon the heels of danger. And still he spoke no word of the sorrow which had brought him to this end.

And Carew, meanwhile, could not fail to note the increasing anxiety with which Alice Mellen wrote of her cousin. From Alice's letters, it appeared that Ethel, totally unnerved by the death of Captain Frazer, had begged so piteously to be released from her hospital work that she had finally been sent home to Cape Town. She had seemed to be far from well, when she had left Johannesburg; nevertheless, she had no sooner reached home than she had plunged into the midst of the whirlpool of social life where she was said to be the gayest of the gay.

Cape Town, that fall, was facing the end of the war and the consequent departure of the swarm of young Englishmen who had made their headquarters there during the past two years. Accordingly, it resolved to make the most of the short time remaining to it; and the early weeks of the year saw the little city neglecting all other things for the sake of making merry with her fast-vanishing heroes. And, in all the round of merry-making, Ethel Dent was in evidence, bright and flashing as the diamonds that blazed on her shoulder, and as soft. Her wit was ceaseless, her energy untiring. Always the middle of a group, she yet always held herself within range of her father's protection. He watched her proudly; yet his pride was sometimes mingled with alarm, as he saw the waxy whiteness of her ears and the dark shadows which lay beneath her eyes. It was plain to him that all was not well with the girl; yet he was wholly at a loss as to the cause of the trouble.

Strange to say, he never once thought of Weldon; neither did his mind linger long upon the Captain. True, Ethel and Captain Frazer had been good friends; but so had Ethel been good friends with many another man. The secret of that last hour of the Captain's life was buried in two hearts. Weldon could not speak of it; Ethel would not. And so, in the eyes of her friends, Ethel's experience had been sorrowful, but scarcely touched with tragedy. The heroic passing of a casual friend is no cause for a lasting change in the nature of a happy-tempered girl.

However, Alice had noted the change and, quite unable to account for it, she had commented upon it to Carew. Her letter, coming that same morning, had quickened his slow-forming resolution to speak. Taken quite by itself, her account of Ethel would have made scant impression upon him. Taken in connection with what he had seen of Weldon, it forced him to draw certain conclusions which, though wrong in detail, were comparatively accurate in their main outlines.

He and Weldon came back from their walk, wrapped in the silence of perfect understanding. Carew had asked few questions; Weldon had made even fewer replies, and those replies had been brief. Ethel's name had scarcely been mentioned between them. Their talk had mainly concerned itself with Captain Frazer, his life, his passing, the void he had left behind him. Only one sentence had related to the scene in the hospital; but its brief, tragic summing up of the situation had been sufficient. Carew had made no answer, save to walk on for a few steps in silence, with his hand resting on the shoulder of his friend.

That night, he wrote to Alice. The letter was long and full of detail. It told what he knew, what he had inferred and what he feared. It begged her, in the name of their own sacred happiness, to help him win the same happiness for these two who, longing to come together, were straying always farther apart; and it ended with the words with which he had begun his talk with Weldon, that noon,--

"For God's sake, how long is this going to last?"

CHAPTER TWENTY-TWO

Paddy waved his thumb disrespectfully towards the rear of the column.

"And what can you expect of a man that goes to the wars in a fancy petticoat, let alone a khaki apron to cover up the front of it?" he demanded. "And look at the bare knees of 'em, for all the world like knots in the branches of an oak-tree! They may be trained to believe it's comfortable to walk round in public with their kneepans in plain sight; but no man can ever make me think it's either beautiful to the eye, or respectful in the presence of one's betters."

"But their officers wear the same uniform, Paddy," Weldon objected. "Who are their betters?"

"Myself, little Canuck, and yourself, too," Paddy answered calmly. "The maple and the shamrock, severally and together, can knock the spots out of all the thistles that's growing."

"Until it comes to a fight," Carew suggested, from Paddy's other side. "The Highlanders have made their record, this time."

But Paddy shook his head. "Wait then till the end of the chapter," he predicted. "My turn hasn't come yet. Belike I'll be the hero of them all. I was minding my pots and my kettles, while the Black Watch was slinging lead up on the road into Kimberley. But, faith, if I was one of them, with the choice before me between a glorious death and the having to live in the sound of the bagpipes, I'd mount a Red Cross and take a white flag in my hand and sally forth to be seen and shot by the Boers."

"You don't like the bagpipes, Paddy?"

Paddy's reply was sententious.

"Did you ever hear a pig soliloquizing to himself, just as he crossed the tracks between the wheels of an express train? Well then!"

"Meanwhile," Carew observed thoughtfully; "I wonder why we are out on this trek."

"To escort the little Canuck with his mounts, and to study the surface of the land, to be sure."

Carew's eye swept the barren, desolate expanse about them.

"It is a bit monotonous, though."

"It's monotony that's healthy. You can't make a whole dinner off from red pepper, and you can't make a whole campaign off from smokeless powder. In either case, you get too much heated up, for the show it all makes. Strike hard and eat hot at long intervals and with exceeding unction; and, meanwhile, pause and let it soak in. It's not the hottest fire that gives off the most blazes. And where is that nigger of a Kruger Bobs?"

"In among the wagons with The Nig." "Just for all the world like the deuce of spades! The Black Watch would better adopt the two of 'em for their colors. The Nig is a pretty bit of property; but this is the brute for me." And Paddy bent over in the saddle to stroke the neck of Piggie who snapped back at him testily.

However, in all truth, the little gray broncho deserved all of Paddy's praise. Scarred from muzzle to pastern by errant bullets, limping slightly on one fore leg, she still had borne her master bravely over weary miles of veldt, into many a skirmish and through the kicking, squealing throngs of her kindred which crowded the Lindley kraal. Long since, Weldon had discovered that the thoroughbred Nig was an ornament; but that Piggie was a necessity. Again and yet again, her flying feet and gritty temper had brought him, unscathed, through perilous plights. She read his mind as by instinct; left unguided, she guided herself with exceeding discretion; and, upon more than one occasion, she had endured the nervous strain of feeling a human body dangling limply above the saddle bow, held in place by main strength of her master who, crouching forward beneath the heavy fire, could only indicate the way of safety by the pressure of this heel and then that against her heaving flanks. Surely, if ever honors could be given to a faithful, plucky little broncho, Piggie should have been gazetted for the Distinguished Service Order. Not to the men alone is due all the honor of victory.

But now Piggie, fresh from a prolonged interval of resting in the care of Kruger Bobs, felt that she was out on an excursion of pure pleasure. Behind her trailed a long column of men and mounts and wagons; around her was a knot of horses whom she knew well; and before her stretched away the dry and level veldt, broken at the sky-line by a range of hills that rose sharply in a jagged line which culminated in one peak lifted far above all the others.

In the very front of the column rode a score or more of the South African Light Horse, with Weldon, for the moment, in command. The man was showing, just then, something of the temper of his mount. It would have been good to leave behind him the slow-moving column and go dashing away alone, far across the level plain. A spirit of restlessness was upon him; Paddy's utterances grew vague in his ears, and he cast longing glances towards the range of hills to the southward, as if eager to explore them and find what secrets, if any, lay within their keeping. Then he reined in his broncho and forced his mind back to Paddy's conversation, still upon the deeds of the kilted heroes of the Black Watch.

"And they do say," he was observing; "that Wauchope was light in his mind-- fey, them piping, petticoated Scotchmen calls it--the night before his death. Now that's something that's beyond my thinking. No dead man ever knows he's going to die. Witness the last words of most of 'em! They make up their death-bed speeches, and then they turn thrifty and save up the speeches till next time. Little Canuck dear, what would you say, if you was hit?"

Weldon laughed shortly.

"I should probably say 'Thank God,'" he answered.

Paddy crossed himself.

"And might heaven forgive you then, little one!" he said gravely. "The Lord and the Holy Virgin may send the bullets to kill you, unless it's from the Boers who is guided by the Father of Lies; but it's small thanks in return they will be asking. Take the benefits of Providence with a shout of thanksgiving; but swallow hard and keep a stiff upper lip, when it smacks you over the head with a shillalegh." Then, of a sudden, he bent over in the saddle once more and rested his hand on Weldon's fingers which lay on the broncho's neck. "And, if I mistake not, little one, it is what you have been doing, these late days, so forgive me teaching you a lesson you've already learned by heart."

Two nights before this, Carew's letter to Alice had ended with the outcry,--

"For God's sake, how long is this going to last?"

And now the end was almost in sight. Early the next day, there had come a call for remounts for a column halted on the veldt near Reitz, and Weldon, with a score of others from his squadron, had been sent out with the mounts to join the column for the trek to the southward. As a matter of course, Weldon had asked that the score might include Paddy and Carew; and now, with them at his side, he was at the head of the column which trailed away far towards the southward, twelve hundred poorly mounted men riding in leisurely fashion towards Harrismith and the chance of rounding up an occasional Boer.

Dusk of the second day had brought the hills on the sky-line close to their eyes, and had sharpened the ragged peaks into threatening crests of bare, black rock. Already the hills were but three miles distant, and the hour for halt almost at hand, when scouts came flying back to the column, breathless with haste and with the consciousness of tidings to impart. The colonel received the tidings with outward calm.

"A laager of fifteen hundred Boers? And a mile and a half to the south of us? We must attack." His eyes swept the faces of his men. "Trooper Weldon?"

At the word, Weldon rode forward and saluted.

"That highest hill is the key to the position. It is the one we must hold. Can you and your men ride around to the west of the laager, get that hill and hold it at all costs until I can send reinforcements to you? The reinforcements will start as soon as you reach the top of the hill. Keep out of sight, while you can. Then rush it. You understand?"

Weldon nodded; then, his head erect, his eyes flashing, he saluted for a second time and, with his men at his heels, dashed off into the thickening dusk.

Like foothills beside a mountain range, so the veldt before him was already broken and crumpled into a series of irregular ridges, opening in their midst to form a tiny plain where the Boer laager lay spread out before them. The dusk of the plain was dotted with scattered camp fires; but, beyond the ridges, it lay heavy, and in that heaviness Weldon placed his trust. For two thirds of his whole distance, he could keep below a ridge to the westward of the laager. The final third lay full in view of the enemy, full up the increasing steepness of the mountain side, where, horses failing, it would be necessary to creep by stealth and upon the hands and knees. And, where the shelter ended, there lay before them a short defile between walls of naked rock, and the defile was narrow.

Half the way to the defile was already accomplished when Weldon heard, from the crest of the ridge above him, the double crack of a Mauser rifle, and then the sound of scurrying, unshod feet. He shut his teeth, and his chin rose a bit higher. "A picket! And now the brute has run in to tell tales," he said shortly. "Quick, men, it's a race between us now."

Answering to the touch of the spur, the gray broncho went leaping forward, with Paddy's horse neck and neck at her side. From beyond the ridge, the trio of guns could be heard, barking ceaselessly, while their shells dropped thick into the laager, scarcely eight hundred yards away. And now the defile, short, but narrow, was close at hand.

Ka-paw! Ka-paw!

From the mouth of the tiny pass, a rain of bullets swept down upon them. A horse dropped, shot through the knee; another, hit in the neck, bolted, threw its wounded rider and then, mad with pain, hurled itself straight into the ranks of the enemy. A second shot, almost at arm's length, threw it to the earth; but not until it had done its work. The half-broken Boer ponies, fat from much feeding and totally unaccustomed to this species of missile, swerved at its approach and destroyed the aim of the second volley, which was answered by a fire that sent a full quarter of the twoscore Boers sprawling heavily groundward.

A scant ten minutes sufficed for the rest. Five troopers lay helpless on the dusty soil. Five dead Boers blocked the trail at the entrance of the narrow pass. It was a drawn game; but the end was not yet. From beyond the ridge, Weldon could hear the guns still pounding ceaselessly. He knew that, half a mile in the rear, his colonel was watching for him to come to the crest of the hill; that, in a sense, the whole game was waiting upon his moves. Whirling himself about, he gave a short, sharp order. Scarcely a moment later, he was astonished to see the Boers in the pass giving way before the mad rush of his paltry fifteen men. The narrow pass was his own.

Beyond the pass were more ridges, some parallel with his course, some crossing it. Far to the eastward, he could see a moving spot, black even in the increasing darkness of the night. Leaving Piggie to pick her own way along the rocky ridge, he rose in his stirrups, shaded his eyes with his hands and peered anxiously towards the spot. At last his straining eyes could make out eight Boer horsemen, riding furiously towards the peak which he was in honor bound to hold. And their course was the chord of the arc of his own circle. He dropped back to the saddle where he bent low, yielding his whole body to the flying body of his horse.

The crest was sharp. To the east, its approach was more easy; but on the west it offered a wall of blank, black rock. The fat Boer ponies were still at some distance from the eastern slope, when Weldon flung himself from his panting broncho. Carew protested, as they told off by fours and he was left, the third man, with Paddy's mount, the gray broncho and a huge brown Argentine horse on his hands.

"Sorry, old man!" Weldon said briefly. "It's luck, and dead against you. Still, it may save Miss Mellen a bad half-hour. Look out for Piggie. She deserves it." And, turning, he led the way up the wall of rock, with thirteen men, breathless, grim and eager, scrambling at his heels.

For moments, it seemed to him that Fate was idly tossing the dice to and fro, before allowing herself to make the final, decisive cast. From the farther side of the hill, he heard a sudden terrified snort from one of the Boer ponies, then the thud of feet, as they charged up the approaches of the long slope. From behind him, there arose a groan, as one of the men, missing his foothold in the deepening dusk, crashed back against the loose rocks at the bottom of the hill. Then a shot and a whinnying moan told him that Carew and his three comrades had edged around the base of the hill into range of the enemy above them. The man might be wounded, too, as well as the mount. Seven Boers, and they were thirteen in all. The cast was all for--

A dash of light! A rattle of firing! Three of his men dropped backwards. The other ten looked up to face a second flash from the summit. Only eight heard the answering echoes which came rolling back to them from the encircling hills. Then Paddy's voice came in his ears, low, but as unconcerned as ever.

"Remember the fellow who was rejected on account of his teeth, little Canuck? 'Faith,' he said; 'it's shooting the damned Boers I want to be, not eating them.' But, by the holy Virgin Mary, in another ten minutes we'll be shaking 'em between our teeth."

The next flash but one showed only five men on the steep rocky wall; but those five men were close to the summit. Once on the top, their rifles could come into play. It was maddening to be picked off, like stuffed crows resting on a tree branch; maddening to listen to the low sounds from beneath which told them that some one of their comrades was facing the end of his fight. Then, just as they reached the summit, one of their five dropped, with a bullet shattering the bone of his ankle.

"Go on, boys! You'll get there," he said, as the next in line dashed past him. "The hill is Weldon's. Mind you hold it for him. The devil is in him, and he's bound to win."

On top of the hill, six Boers were huddled in the scant shelter of a few low, scattered rocks tufted with a bunch of brush whose bleached stalks marked the darkness with a pale line of range for their fire. The next volley went astray. It was answered by the crack of Paddy's rifle. Paddy's chuckle followed close on the crack. "I rolled him over like a sausage in the hot fat," he commented, as he took a second aim. "Here goes for another, and may his bed in heaven have a valance to hide his sins!" A second Boer vanished behind the rocks.

Four Boers in shelter, four Britons in the open; and, on the plain beneath, twenty-seven hundred men were waiting to see the outcome of the game.

The tension of the eight men increased. It rendered their aim unsteady. Under its influence, seven men fell to wasting their ammunition. The eighth was Paddy. Firing rarely, his rare bullets told. Now a finger was shattered, now an ear was grazed.

"I'm not doing much killing; but, faith, I'm warming 'em up a bit," he said, as he halted to cool his rifle. "It's keeping the ball a- rolling, and them busy. Else, belike they'd find Satan filling the idle hands of them with bad deeds. Little Canuck dear, this is hot work for a boy."

Weldon nodded. His hat had been lost in the scramble up the hill, his putties were dragged into heaps of khaki about his knees, the shoulder of his coat was torn by a passing bullet and a scarlet trickle lined his cheek; but his face was alert and eager, his lips parted in a half-smile which brought back to Paddy's mind a dim picture of the boyish trooper he had known and loved at Piquetberg Road. Then another man in khaki dropped at their feet. The lines of Weldon's mouth straightened.

"No go," he said briefly. "We must charge. It's our only chance."

Paddy took one last, hasty shot. Then, gripping his rifle, he turned to Weldon.

"True, little Canuck," he answered loyally. "Go on, and be sure Paddy will follow you to the other edge of the grave!"

He spoke truthfully. The reinforcements came rushing up the eastern slope of the hill, to find their pathway encumbered with bearded men in frock-coats and bandoliers. On top of the crest, surrounded by the wounded and the dying, sat a single man in khaki, the light of victory in his gleaming eyes, and Paddy's lifeless body clasped in his weary arms.

CHAPTER TWENTY-THREE

"Yes," Carew said meditatively; "I wish there had been glory enough to go around. As long as there wasn't, though, I am glad it was fated to fall to your share."

Weldon hurled a little black stone at a great black rock.

"Not so much glory, after all."

Carew raised his eyes and apostrophized the dark gray clouds rushing across the paler gray arch of the sky.

"Just listen to the man! What can he be wanting? 'Not so much glory!' And he recommended for a V. C.!"

Weldon shook his head.

"What does it profit a man," he paraphrased; "if he gain the V. C. and lose one of his best friends? Besides, I didn't gain it; it was fated. Paddy was as brave as I, and so were half a dozen more of them. It was only chance that brought me through the bullets."

"Poor Paddy!" Carew's tone was full of thoughtful regret.

"Not poor at all. He had the end we all are wishing for. He died with his boots on, and fighting pluckily for a forlorn hope. We can't mourn a man that we envy."

Half way to the distant sky-line, the horses of the squadron were grazing peacefully over the stubbly grass. The corporal and the third of the troopers appointed to guard them were far away towards the crest of a ridge to the westward, and Carew and Weldon were alone. Carew sat silent for a moment, his eyes on the scattered groups of horses. Then he turned and looked directly at his friend.

"Perhaps," he assented. "I was sorry to be out of the scrimmage. It took all my grit to obey you, old man; but it was an order. Now it is over--"

"Well?" Weldon prompted him.

"Now it is over, I am less sorry than I was. The fact is, the future holds a good deal for us."

"For you, perhaps."

"For you, too. The whole future of a man doesn't go to wreck in an hour. There are other crises later on, and some of them are bound to come out well. Save yourself for those, Weldon. There is no especial use in throwing yourself away."

"I'm not. But, when the order comes, I must obey it," Weldon said gloomily.

"It depends something on the order; but it depends a good sight more on the way you obey it. When a man comes into collision with a bulldog, it's generally wise to grapple with him back of his teeth; else, you may lose a thumb or two. It's the same way with your orders here. Because you don't funk, there is no reason you should flirt with an early death."

"But I don't."

"What about now?"

"What do you mean?"

"That you ought to be in hospital."

Weldon threw back his head and laughed, but mirthlessly.

"Why, then?"

Without speaking, Carew took out his pipe, filled it and began fumbling in his pocket.

"Have you a match?" he asked.

Weldon nodded, produced the match, lighted it and held it to the extended pipe. Carew's eyes, drooped to the bowl, watched the bit of flame.

"Do you call that a steady hand?" he asked then. "Man, you're ill, I tell you. Your face is hot and your hands are cold, and your nerves are worn to shoestrings, frayed shoestrings at that. If you keep on, you'll be down flatter than you like. You ought to have stopped four weeks ago."

Weldon crossed his arms at the nape of his neck and lay back at his ease on the ground.

"Then what would have become of my V. C.?" he queried, with languid indifference.

"But I thought you claimed not to care for your V. C."

"I don't. My friends may, however." "As a legacy? I think your friends may possibly choose you to the V. C."

"Foolish of them," Weldon commented. "Still, 'If we could choose the time, and choose aright, 'T were best to die, our honor at the height.' I learned that when I was a small boy; but I've only just found out what it means."

With scoffing lips, but eyes full of unspoken love, Carew turned on his friend.

"Don't dodder, Weldon," he counselled him. "That's canting drivvle, made to console the unsuccessful. No man knows when he has reached his high-water mark. Yours may have come on the day you licked Stevie Ballard for gilding the tailless cat; it may not come till you are ninety."

"No." The syllable was quiet, deliberate. Then Weldon roused himself and sat up to speak with sudden energy. "Promise me this, Carew, that while the matter is hanging fire, you won't mention this V. C. business to any one."

Carew stared at him in unmixed surprise.

"What's the matter now?" he asked blankly.

"Nothing, only that I want you to promise."

"Not to--"

"Not to a living soul."

"Why? What's the use?"

"No use, but my wish. If it comes off, let it be as a joyous surprise. If it misses fire, as it quite well may, then there'll be no harm done. In either case, it is best to keep still. My own notion is that I'll not get it. As a rule, one doesn't get the V. C. for shinning up the side of a hill, no matter how steep it is."

Carew made no attempt to discuss the chances. Instead, he merely asked,--

"Mayn't I tell Miss Mellen?"

Weldon shook his head. It was exactly to prevent the inevitable consequences of Alice Mellen's knowing the story that he was seeking to extort the promise from Carew. To protect his motive, however, he took a sudden resolution.

"I shall not even tell my mother," he answered, with slow emphasis.

Carew raised his brows.

"Then I suppose that ties my tongue. I am sorry. What's the use of being so confoundedly modest, Weldon?"

"Do you promise?"

"I suppose I must."

"On your honor?"

"On my honor."

Weldon stretched himself out at full length once more.

"So be it. Give me a light. You took my last match," he said as unconcernedly as if they had merely been talking of the weather.

Indeed, the weather might well have been the subject of their talk. The earth was baked until it cracked beneath the parching sun and wind. There had been no rain for weeks; but, to-day, the raw wind sent the lead-colored clouds flying over the sky, and the lead- colored clouds were heavy with rain. All the morning and till mid- afternoon, the column had been camping not far away, while their weary, hungry mounts had been turned out on the veldt to graze. For men and mounts, the halt was needed.

The fight about the laager had been no easy victory. Twelve hundred half-starved Britons are no match for fifteen hundred Boers fat with easy living. Weldon's hold on the crest had decided the game; but the game had not played itself out without wounds for some and utter weariness for all. War mad, yet half-dazed in all other respects, Weldon had watched the reinforcements come swarming up the hill to his relief, had heard their cheers mingling themselves with the sound of his name. Then, listless, but with his arm still about Paddy's shoulders, he had seen the fight move to its destined finish. He came down from the hilltop, feeling that something had taken yet one more turn in the evertightening coil of his brain. For one instant, as they were laying Paddy into the narrow grave scooped out of the veldt, the coil relaxed. Then, as the lumps of earth closed over his plucky, loyal little comrade, it tightened again and pressed on him more closely than ever.

And that was a week ago; and the week between had been one long trek in search of errant Boers. Weldon still rode in the front of the column. He had been ordered into hospital; but, bracing himself, he had looked the doctor steadily between the eyes and had refused to obey. The hospital was not for him--as yet. "By Jove!" Carew was remarking deliberately. "Look at the horses!"

Noses in air, tails lashing and eyes staring wildly, the frightened groups had swept together and were rushing down upon them in one mad stampede. Straight towards the two troopers they came dashing along, swerved slightly and went sweeping past them, wrapped in a thick column of dust which parted, just as the horde rushed by, before the fierce impact of the breaking storm. From zenith to horizon, the leaden sky was marked with wavering lines of golden fire; but the shock of the thunder was outborne by the clash of falling hail. Half a mile away, the tents were riddled by the egg-sized lumps of ice; and, out on the open veldt, Carew threw himself on the earth, face downward, and buried his head in his sheltering arms. But Weldon staggered to his feet. In the thick of the flying troop of horses, he had seen the little gray broncho, and now, before she swept on out of hearing, he turned his back to the gale and gave a high, shrill whistle. It was months, now, since Piggie had learned that call. Again and again she had come trotting up to him, to rub her muzzle against his neck in token that she had heard and understood. There was scant chance that the call would be carried to her by the boisterous wind, scanter chance still that, hearing it now in that mad rout, she would heed. Nevertheless, Weldon took the chance. Obviously stampeded by the enemy, the missing horses would leave the column powerless to repel the attack which was imminent. If Piggie could be recalled, there was still a chance to regain the other mounts. Yet, even while he was weighing all the chances, he smiled to himself as he recalled the ineffectual little whistle that had gone out on the whistling wind. The chance was gone. Like Carew, he would lie down and seek what shelter he could get from the earth and from his own clasping arms.

The hail, falling thickly, shut down about the troop of horses and took them from his sight. If his eyes could have followed them, he would have seen one little gray head toss itself upward from the heart of the throng, one sturdy little gray back move more and more slowly, turn slightly, then weave its patient way in and out between its frightened companions until, free from the press of the crowd, it stood alone on the hail-lashed plain. Ten minutes later, Weldon felt a soft, wet muzzle poking its way between his tight-locked arms. The rest was simple. It amounted to riding back to the column to give warning of the enemy who rode close in the rear, to summoning Kruger Bobs and The Nig, and then, without stopping for a saddle, to go galloping away to the sky-line to round up the stampeded herd. The first dash of hail over, the rain fell fast upon them; but, above its roar, they could hear the steady firing of the pom pom behind them and the crackle of musketry mingled with the heavier fire.

Four o'clock had brought the stampede and the storm. Seven o'clock brought Weldon and Kruger Bobs, drenched to the skin, back into a demoralized camp. Nine o'clock found Weldon still in the saddle, his teeth chattering, his brown cheeks ablaze and his eyes hot with fever, while he waited for the pitching of his tattered tent. Then, even before its soggy, torn folds were stretched and pegged into position, he turned and rode off in search of a doctor.

"Sorry," he said briefly; "but I think I've a touch of fever. Can you put me to bed somewhere?"

The next morning, he greeted Kruger Bobs by the name of a girl cousin who had died, ten years before.

CHAPTER TWENTY-FOUR

For two weeks, the fever held Weldon in its grip. For two weeks, he was prostrate, first with the halting column, then at the base hospital at Kroonstad. The fever was never very high, nor was it intermittent. It merely hung about him and ate away his strength. For the time being, he was content to lie quiet and stare up at the electric lights scattered through the tent and wonder about Ethel. Now and then some sight in the hospital set him to thinking about the Captain, wondering if he were happy in his new life of rest and peace, he who had so often been in the thick of the fiercest fight. Or he thought of Paddy, brave, merry little Irishman who, fighting like an angry wolf, had died with a joke still hanging on his lips. Then his mind went back again to Ethel.

In vain they urged him to sleep; in vain they gave him bromides. The body was at rest; but the wheels of the brain whirred as busily as ever, and as logically. No hint of delirium mingled with his thought processes. It might have saved something if there had.

Then, one day, Weldon sat up for an hour. The next day, he was put into his clothes and, three days later, supported on the strong arm of Kruger Bobs, he crawled into a hospital train bound for Cape Town. It was an order, and he obeyed. Nevertheless, he shrank from the very mention of Cape Town. It had been the core of his universe; but now the core had gone bad. But his time of service had expired. Red tape demanded that he receive the papers for his discharge from the Cape Town citadel. That done, he would take the first outgoing steamer for London. Afterwards, he would leave his life in the hands of Fate. He took no note of the fact that Fate might step into the game earlier than he then foresaw.

For full seven hundred miles, the train lumbered on to the southward. It was tedious, exhausting; yet Weldon found a certain interest in the jar of the rolling wheels to which he fitted the measure of his whirring thoughts. As long as the rhythm of the wheels lasted, his thoughts slowed down to meet their time. When the train halted, his thoughts dashed off again; but they resumed their slower course as soon as the wheels began once more. He took no note of the country about him, as they passed from veldt to karroo, from karroo to the coast plateau, and from the coast plateau down across the Cape Flats, sparsely covered with pipe grass and acacias. Then, as Table Mountain and the Devil's Peak lifted themselves on his right hand, he knew that Cape Town was near, and he braced himself to go through what was before him.

Kruger Bobs eyed him anxiously.

"Boss sick," he announced for the dozenth time, as the train drew in at the Adderley Street station. "Boss berry sick mans. Boss go hotel soon."

But Weldon shook his head. Even now, rest had scant space in his plans, least of all, rest in Cape Town.

"I can do it," he asserted resolutely. "Steady me till I get started, Kruger Bobs. Then I shall astonish you by my agility."

"Boss go hotel," Kruger Bobs muttered in low-voiced mutiny. "Boss too sick to trek."

"No fear. Did you ever know me to give out, when there was something still to be done, Kruger Bobs?"

"What Boss do?"

"My discharge. My banker. My passage home."

The arm of Kruger Bobs tightened about the bony figure of his master, but the pressure of his strong arm was only gentle and reassuring, and the great, white-ringed eyes glittered wet. This was not the boy master to whom Kruger Bobs had sworn allegiance. This was an older man, and weak withal. But the weaker grew the master, the stronger grew the loyal, loving allegiance of the man.

After the wide, deserted stretches of open veldt, the roar of Adderley Street seemed to Weldon like the maddening tumult of Piccadilly. The noise stunned him; the hurrying crowd filled him with terror. Even inside the cab, he still clung to the arm of the faithful Kruger Bobs. Still clinging to that faithful arm, he came out from the citadel, no longer Trooper Weldon, but Mr. Harvard Weldon once more, honorably discharged from the South African Light Horse. Kruger Bobs was invisible behind the spreading limits of his smile; but Weldon had scarcely heeded the words which had been addressed to him. All at once, like a watch about to run down, the wheels of his brain were moving slowly and ever more slowly. His whole resolution now centered in keeping them in motion long enough to go to his banker and to the office of the steamship company. Once on the steamer and sliding out across Table Bay, he could leave the rest to the ship's doctor and to Fate.

Even in the multitude of strangers who had passed through Cape Town, in those latter months, he was remembered at the bank and greeted with a word of congratulation on his record in the field. At the word, a man beside him, hearing, turned to look, looked again, and then held out his hand. It was the father of Ethel Dent.

That night, the Dents dined alone. Over the roast, Mr. Dent looked up suddenly.

"Whom do you think I saw, to-day, Ethel?"

"Who now?" she asked, smiling. "You can't expect me to guess, when you are constantly running up against the most impossible people." "Not this time. It was quite possible; but it gave me a shock. It was Mr. Weldon."

The smile died from her lips. Nevertheless, she asked, with a forced lightness,--

"What shocked you?"

"His looks. He was ghastly, thin to a shadow and burning up with fever. I was in the bank, and I heard some one speak his name; but I had to look at him for a second time, before I could recognize him. The man is a wreck. He looked sixty years old, as he went crawling off, on the arm of his Kaffir boy. I'm sorry. I always liked Weldon."

A bit of bread lay by Ethel's plate. For an instant, her finger tips vanished inside its yielding surface. Then she looked up.

"Too bad! He was a good fellow," she said quietly. Then she lifted her hand to her throat. "Dear me! Have I lost my diamond pin?" she added hastily. "I was sure I put it on. Please excuse me, while I see if I left it in my room." And she ran swiftly out of the room.

Mrs. Dent broke the pause.

"Where was Mr. Weldon going?"

"To his hotel. I came out, just as they drove away, and I heard the boy give the order to the driver."

"Which hotel was it?"

"I--Really, I don't remember. He used to go to the Grand."

"He seemed ill?"

"He seemed--" For an instant, Mr. Dent held the word in suspension. Then he let it drop with a slow quietness which added tenfold to its weight--"dead."

His wife's gentle eyes clouded.

"I am sorry. I liked the boy. He was good to me."

"I had thought Ethel liked him, too," her husband added a little inconsequently.

"So she did in a way. But there have been so many others." The mother sighed slightly. In her young days, there had been but one. Now, remembering that one and watching him in the present, she found it hard to comprehend Ethel's free-handed distribution of social favors among so great a throng of admirers. There had always been many; now, since her recent return from Johannesburg, the many had become a multitude, and each of the multitude could show proof of her liking. But Mrs. Dent recurred to the fact of Weldon's illness.

"Poor boy! Fancy being really ill, so far from home and in a hotel!" she added slowly.

"It is one of the risks of a soldier," her husband reminded her.

"Yes, and the soldiers fought for us. Where would your mines have been without them?" she suggested in return. "I really wish you would telephone to the hotel and find out something more definite about him."

Her husband looked covetously at the entree, just appearing in sight.

"Now?" he asked.

She ignored the mockery of his tone.

"Yes, please," she assented quietly. "It will only take you a minute."

It took him ten. When he came back into the room, his hat was in his hand.

"I think I will go over to the Grand for a minute," he explained. "I don't quite like what I hear."

"What did you hear?"

In the dim upper hallway, a girlish figure leaned far over the railing and strained her ears for the reply. Then, noiselessly, the door of her room shut again behind her.

"They tell me," Mr. Dent was saying; "that Weldon is there, unconscious in his room. The boy brought him into the house in his arms, and they have sent for Dr. Wright. It is a bad case of enteric, mixed with some trouble with the brain. He appears to be suffering from nervous shock, they say, increased by a long strain of anxiety."

Half an hour later, he was called from Weldon's room to speak to his wife at the telephone.

"Yes," he answered her. "It is as bad as I heard, as bad as it can be. You think so? Are you strong enough? Sure? Hold the wire, then, till I ask the doctor." The interval was short; and he went on again, "The doctor says he can be moved now, but not later. It may be a matter of weeks. How soon can you be ready? Very well. Will you be sure to save yourself all you can? In an hour, then. And the doctor will have a nurse waiting there? And can you put the boy into some corner? He would be frantic, if we tried to leave him behind. Very well. Yes." And the telephone rang off.

It was midnight before the Dent household was fully reconstructed. Upstairs in the great eastern front room, a white-capped nurse was bending above the unconscious man in the bed; downstairs in the kitchen, the tears of Kruger Bobs were mingling with the cold roast beef on the table before him. The doctor had just gone away, and in the room underneath the sickroom, Mr. Dent and his wife were quietly laying plans to meet the needs of the changed routine which had fallen upon their home. He looked up, as Ethel came slowly into the room.

"By the way, Ethel, I forgot to ask you before; but did you find your pin?"

She looked at him wonderingly. Her face was pale and drawn; but her eyes were shining like the gems she had professed to miss.

"What pin do you mean?" she asked blankly.

CHAPTER TWENTY-FIVE

"Don't wait any longer, Carew. Really, it's not worth while."

"Too late for us to part company now," Carew answered serenely.

"I know. You've stood by me like a good fellow; but it will be some time yet before I can sail. And you know you are in a hurry to get away."

"Don't be too sure of that," Carew advised him. "All my good things aren't at one end of the world."

Weldon's lips curled into the ghost of his old smile.

"Then take one of them along with you," he suggested.

Elbows on knees and chin on fists joined knuckle to knuckle, Carew turned and smiled blandly down at the face on the pillow.

"Weldon, for a man who has been off his head for a month, you do have singularly wise ideas. But do you suppose she'd go?"

"Which?"

"Miss Mellen, of course. It's a question of ages. Young Mahomet is easier to move than the everlasting hills."

"Meaning your mother? She would thank you." "She will thank me, when she sees Alice," Carew responded hopefully. "But, honor bright, do you suppose Miss Mellen would go back with me?"

"I thought she promised."

"Yes, but now," Carew persisted, with the eagerness of a boy. "Right off, next month."

"There's only one way to tell; ask her," Weldon answered. "If she is the girl I think she is, she will say yes."

"You do like her; don't you, Weldon?" The eagerness was still in his tone.

"Intensely," Weldon replied quietly. "I have seen few women I have liked as well."

"What larks we'll be having, this time next year, talking it all over together," Carew said, in a sudden, thoughtful burst of prophecy. "By the time we get home, we shall forget the blood and the dog-biscuit, and only remember the skittles and beer. If only--"

"What?" Weldon looked up at him without flinching.

Carew did flinch, however.

"Nothing," he said hastily. "One is never quite content, you know."

Weldon drew a deep, slow breath.

"No," he echoed. "One is never quite content."

Carew crossed his legs, as he settled back in his chair.

"Mayhap. Some of us ought to be, though."

"Yes. You're a lucky fellow, Carew."

"So are you. The trouble is, one never knows when he is well off."

"But we all know when we aren't," Weldon replied succinctly.

Carew's glance was expressive, as it roved about the luxurious room, with the bed drawn up near the window which looked out, between the branches of an ancient oak tree, on the blue waters of Table Bay and on the fringe of shipping by the Docks far to the eastward. Faintly from the room below came the sound of a piano and of a hushed girlish voice singing softly to itself.

"It all depends on one's point of view," Carew said, after an interval. "I am living in a seven-by-nine room in a hotel, and Miss Mellen is seventy-two miles and three quarters away. Weldon, you are a lucky dog, if you did but know it."

Weldon shut his teeth for a moment. Then he said quietly,--

"Carew, it is five weeks that I have been in this house. Mr. Dent and dear little Mother Dent have been angel-good to me. Miss Dent--" He hesitated.

"Has been an archangel?" Carew supplemented calmly.

"Has never once come into my sight."

Deliberately, forcefully, the next words dropped from Carew's tongue. "The--devil--she--hasn't!"

"No."

Then Weldon waited for Carew to speak; but Carew merely sat and stared at his friend in speechless stupefaction.

"Oh, Lord!" he blurted out at last. "Then you haven't made it up?"

"There was nothing to make up," Weldon said drearily.

Again Carew's elbows came down on his knees with a bump.

"There was, too!" he contradicted, with an explosiveness which irresistibly reminded Weldon of their kindergarten days.

"What makes you think so?"

"I don't think. I know."

"How do you know?" Weldon asked listlessly.

"Alice Mellen told me," Carew replied conclusively.

"Told you what?"

"That Cooee Dent is in love with you."

From his superior knowledge, Weldon stared disdainfully up at him.

"Then there is one thing that Alice Mellen doesn't know."

"She does, then. She told me about it, when you went off on your feed, up at Lindley," Carew explained hurriedly. "I was worried about you, and she was worried about Miss Dent, and we compared notes. You hadn't said a word of any kind; we could only guess at things, so we wrote to each other about it. She told me then about Miss Dent's dashing up to Johannesburg after Vlaakfontein."

"She went to see her cousin."

"She also went to see you."

Carew's emphatic pause was broken by the coming of the nurse, who bent over the bed, raising her brows inquiringly, as she laid two fingers on Weldon's wrist. Carew took the obvious hint.

"I hope I've not stopped too long," he said, as he rose. "It has been good to see Mr. Weldon. May I come again?"

The nurse was a true woman. Therefore she smiled back into his happy, handsome face.

"I think you may," she answered. "Mr. Weldon is tired now, but you evidently have done him good."

Carew meditated aloud, as he went away down the walk.

"Out of every five women, three are cats," he observed tranquilly to himself. "I've cornered the fourth. It remains to be seen whether Weldon is cornered by the fifth, or only the third. Hasn't been to see him! Little beast! But I'll bet any amount of gold money that she has done endless messing for him on the sly."

Carew's words showed that it is usually not the man in love with a woman who is the shrewdest judge of the hidden recesses of that woman's nature. The fact was, Ethel had slaved unceasingly, but unseen, for the patient above stairs. See him she would not. Day after day, she invented fresh excuses to ward off her mother's suggestions of a call on the invalid; but also, day by day, she invented fresh delicacies to tempt the appetite dulled by months of army biscuit and bully beef. And, meanwhile, she was waiting.

Rather to her surprise, no message came down to her from the invalid's room.

She had supposed as a matter of course that Weldon would intuitively recognize the source of the dainties which reached him anonymously. Man-fashion, however, he could see no reason that his beef tea and his wine jelly should be the work of different hands. He devoured them both, and reflected thankfully upon the skill of the Kaffir cook. Mr. Dent had been scrupulously literal in carrying out the commands laid upon him by his daughter. He had left in Weldon's mind no doubt whatsoever about the truth of his statement that Mrs. Dent alone had been responsible for the invalid's present quarters. Weldon had lavished thanks upon Mrs. Dent, and she had received them without demur, as her own lawful property. Even now, he was at a loss whether his recovery was more owing to Mrs. Dent or to the nurse. Each had given to him a large share of her vitality.

From a distance, he could follow Ethel's doings, could assure himself that his presence was no apparent check upon her happiness. Now it was the muffled whirr of the bell, followed by low voices from the room beneath. Now it was the roll of the carriage, bearing her away to dine or to dance, and leaving Weldon to lie and count the minutes until she returned. Now it was her light footstep on the stairs, or, but this was only at long intervals, her hushed voice in the hallway outside his door. At first, he used to lie and hold his breath, while he waited for her to open the door of his room. By degrees, however, he ceased to expect her. And, as the expectation died away, he chafed increasingly at the slowness of his recovery. Anything to get out of that house! She treated him as he would have scorned to treat an invalid dog who had taken refuge in his stable.

All this came slowly. For two endless weeks, Weldon lay unconscious. For two more endless weeks, he raved in delirium. Happily, his nurse was a discreet woman. She discouraged the visits of Mrs. Dent and her husband, offered the excuse that strange faces excited the invalid, and only admitted them during his brief intervals of sleep. Meanwhile, she used all her professional principles to keep herself from trying to solve the problem before her eyes. Upstairs was a man sick unto death, a man who raved ceaselessly of the daughter of the house. Downstairs, the daughter of the house was going her accustomed way, with never a question in regard to the man above. What had happened? How, if anything had happened, how did he chance to be in that home, with Mrs. Dent as his devoted and anxious slave? Resolutely, she fell to studying her temperature charts. Her specialty was fever, not heart disease.

A week after the tide had turned, Carew had been allowed to spend a short half-hour with the invalid. The next day, by advice of the nurse, Mr. Dent telephoned to him to come again. Something, whether in his personality or in his talk, had been of tonic power over Weldon. It seemed wise to repeat the experiment.

Carew came on the heels of his own voice through the telephone; and his face was smiling broadly, as he went leaping up the stairs. After all, it had not been in vain, his quixotic lingering in Cape Town for a weary month after receiving his discharge. Weldon and he had been good friends through thick and thin; it would have been beastly to leave him. And now, after all these useless weeks, he could at least do something to lighten the convalescence. Moreover, Carew's pocket held three letters, received that very noon; one of grudging approval from his son-sick mother, one of chaotic, but heartfelt thanks from Mrs. Weldon, and the third one an affirmative answer to a telegram he had sent to Alice Mellen, only the night before. He went into Weldon's room, looking, as he felt, the embodiment of happiness and health.

He hailed Weldon from the threshold. Tidings like his could wait during no interchange of mere conventional greetings. Weldon heard him to the end, congratulated him, demanded the repetition of all the details. Then, when Carew's excitement had quite spent itself, Weldon drew a letter from underneath his pillow.

"It came, this morning," he added laconically.

Carew seized the letter and ran his eye down the page. Then his face lighted.

"Nunc dimittis!" he said piously. "It's sure to be yours! Have you told Miss Dent?"

"I've not seen Miss Dent."

Carew's face fell.

"Not yet? But you will. And then you will tell her?"

Weldon's lips straightened into a thin line. He shook his head.

"But she ought to know."

"Why?"

"It is her right."

"Why?" Weldon asked again.

"Because--it is. It might make some difference in--"

Weldon stopped him abruptly.

"It could make no difference, Carew. In facing the main question, such things as that don't count. Even if they did, though," he rose on his elbow and faced his friend steadily; "even if they did, I would never consent to try to bribe a girl into loving me, by telling her I had won the V. C. It will be time enough for Miss Dent to hear of it, when it is given."

"But you will be in England then," Carew objected practically.

Weldon lay down again and drew the sheet upward till its shadow lay across his lips.

"What matter?" he answered slowly. "And, besides, Miss Dent isn't the girl to be won in any such way as that. Hers is a love to be given, not bought."

Half an hour later, Carew met Ethel on the stairs. As he halted to speak to her, he was shocked at the look in her face. The lips were smiling; but the eyes were the eyes of a hunted animal.

"So long since we have met!" he said, as he took her hand. "And so much has happened."

"Yes. I have been hoping to congratulate you," she answered.

"It was a stunning letter you wrote me," he said boyishly. "I suppose we are cousins now."

Then there came a little pause. Before either of them quite realized it, the pause had lengthened until it was hard to break.

"I have been up to see the invalid," he blurted out at last.

"How is he?" the girl inquired courteously.

"Better." Then a sudden note of resentment crept into Carew's honest voice. "He is counting the days now before he can be moved. He says your mother has been wonderfully good to him."

The girl stood aside to let Carew pass her by.

"She is good to everybody," she assented quietly. "I hope Mr. Weldon won't think of going away until he can be moved with perfect safety. It is really no trouble to have him here, and the nurse is very capable."

And Carew bowed in agreement. Once outside the door, however, he freed his mind, tersely and with vigor.

"Damn the nurse!" he said to the oak tree, as he passed it.

CHAPTER TWENTY-SIX

"There's a true Heart in the West World, that is beating still for me, Ever praying in the twilight once again my face to see. Oh, the World is good and gladsome, with its Love both East and West, But there's ever one love only that is still the First and Best."

The low voice died away. A moment later, Ethel Dent pushed open one of the long windows of the drawing-room and stepped out on the veranda. The flower-boxes were filled with limp stalks, chilled by the frost of the previous night; but the sun lay warm over the wide, white steps, over the lawn and over the bay beyond. She stood for a moment, staring thoughtfully out across the bay; then she moved on to the western end of the veranda, looked up at Table Mountain with its cloth of cloud, and then dropped down into one of the chairs which still remained in the sunny corner.

That corner held many memories for her. She had sought it now unconsciously; yet, once there, she lingered, although for weeks past she had been seeking to banish those memories from her life. Why keep them? They belonged to a chapter that was dead and gone. Better to seal its pages and never break the seal. Better never to reread what had been written there. If she had been mistaken in giving her love where it was not desired, not only should the world never be aware of the fact; but she herself would ignore the existence of that mistake. She had loved Weldon with all the energy of her headstrong, girlish nature. She had supposed that he had loved her in return. Instead of that, he had gone away and left her without a word, just when her need for him was the greatest. No man in his senses could have seen the agony of that last hour she had spent with Captain Frazer, and failed to understand the pitiful, appealing look she had cast upon him. Unable to escape the agony, she had given this tacit call to Weldon to share it with her, to understand, and to forgive. She had been sure she could trust him; but it was evident that she had trusted him in vain. In the hour of her supremest need, he had gone away and left her alone. No man who cared for her could have forsaken her in such a crisis as that. Her lips curved into a hard little smile, as she sat rocking to and fro in the sunshine, and, going back over a past which she had rarely allowed herself to reopen.

And afterwards? Afterwards Fate had been all against her. It had been easy to escape from her engagement at Johannesburg, comparatively easy to shut the past experience into the inner places of her mind, to close her lips with the show of a smile, and to plunge into a whirl of social life which should leave her no time for quiet thought. So long as she kept her secret to herself, it mattered nothing to the girl that it was eating pitilessly at her vitality, that it was ever hard and harder for her to keep up her ceaseless round of gayety.

And then, all at once, their home life had been invaded by the man who was never absent from her thoughts. In a sense, she was glad of the invasion. It proved to her, more surely than any words could have done, that she had kept her secret well and beyond suspicion. Had her mother gained any inkling of the true state of the case, Harvard Weldon would never have been brought away from the room at the Grand. For so much surety, Ethel Dent could rejoice with a thankful heart. Nevertheless, as the days passed by, Weldon's presence in the house increased the strain tenfold. Night after night, Ethel had crept noiselessly from her room across the hallway and crouched outside his door, listening for any sounds from within which might tell her that all was well with the man whom she would not see. Day after day, she forced her life to run along in its usual grooves, going out of the house with a laugh on her lips and, in her heart, the sickening dread of the tidings which might greet her upon her return. Again and again, as she passed the door left open during the nurse's temporary absence from the room, she put forth all her strength to keep herself from stealing in, to look just once on the unconscious face of the man who had made her whole life. But she held herself in check, and never once yielded to the temptation. Well she might hold herself in check. She realized only too keenly that, once face to face with Weldon, she would have to do over again all the weary work of those weeks of self- repression.

Then the stupor had given place to delirium; and, even in her room and behind her closed door, she could hear the low, muttering voice. After that, she crouched no more outside his room. It would have been impossible for her to say just what it was that she dreaded to hear. Nevertheless, she closed her ears as resolutely as she closed her door; but, when she met the nurse on the stairs, she hurried onward with her face turned away and her cheeks ablaze.

And then in its turn the delirium had ended. From that time forward, Ethel went out more constantly than ever. When she was in the house, she started and grew red or pale at every unexpected step. Now, at any hour, there might come a summons for her to go to the invalid's room. She went over in detail every possible reply she could make to every possible word which Weldon might say. She held herself ready for any emergency. But the days dragged away, and no emergency had come.

And then, as it had chanced, she had been away from home, when Weldon had finally left the house. It had been the fulfilment of an old promise which had taken her to spend two days with a friend in Newlands. She had had no notion that the time for Weldon's going away was at hand. Neither, on the other hand, had Weldon any idea that Ethel was absent from home. He had merely taken advantage of the first day when the doctor had ceased to oppose his removal. It had been to him a cruel disappointment that Mrs. Dent had stood alone on the steps to watch his departure.

That was three weeks before. Ethel had supposed that Weldon would sail for home at once. He had supposed so, too, until all at once he had found it impossible to turn his back upon Cape Town and all it held. Deep down in his heart was the memory of Carew's words, assuring him of the reason of Ethel's sudden journey to Johannesburg after the fight at Vlaakfontein. The episode was now far away in the past. It might chance, however, that something of the old mood might linger in her mind. Carew had felt sure of her love for him. Perhaps she had loved him once, before the Captain had won the first place in her heart. Perhaps--He had grown dizzy and had grasped the edge of the pillow to steady himself, the first time the idea had dawned upon him--Perhaps, now that the Captain had gone beyond the reach of human love, he might win her to care for himself once more. The chance appeared to him to be wellnigh impossible; yet, while it lingered in his mind, he could not force himself to go away from Cape Town.

The worst of his convalescence was ended, before he was allowed to leave the Dents' home. He strained every nerve to hasten his full recovery. The path of Ethel Dent was not parallel to the course of any semi-invalid. If he were to meet her at all, it must be as a man in full health. By degrees, the color came back to his face, his lean figure lost something of its lankness, his tread grew firmer and more alert. But the old shadow still lingered in his eyes; the strained lines about his lips did not relax. Weldon's mental healing kept no pace with his physical one.

By degrees, too, his table littered itself with cards of invitation. As yet, he felt himself too weak for any but the most informal functions; and Carew, always at his elbow, assured him from his own experience that informality, just then, was an unknown word in the social vocabulary of Cape Town. Carew, bidden on all sides, was dividing his time between his convalescent friend and the gayeties of early winter. He dined and danced almost without ceasing; and, in the intervals of his dining and dancing, he told over to Weldon all the details of his social career. And these details largely concerned themselves with Ethel Dent: how she looked, what she wore, what she said, with whom she danced and with whom she sat it out. And, as he listened, Weldon made up his mind that, for him, the time for resting at home was ended. It was better, easier to go to see for himself than it was to sit at home and imagine things, or to hear about them, after they had happened. There was to be a reception at the Citadel, next week. He would begin with that.

One resolution led to the next. Only two days after he had determined upon the reception, he ordered Kruger Bobs to saddle the gray broncho and to attend him upon The Nig. Then, when the noon sun lay warm over the city, he mounted and, with Kruger Bobs behind him, he rode slowly down Adderley Street to the water front, and turned eastward to the home of the Dents.

The wide veranda and the great white pillars seemed like home to him, in all truth. That house had been the scene of some of his best hours, as of his worst ones, and his heart pounded madly against his ribs as he caught sight of its familiar outlines. Then he drew in his breath sharply and bore down hard in his stirrups, while his face went white to the lips. From the western end of the veranda a girlish figure had risen, halted for a moment with the sun beating full upon her vivid hair; then, heedless of the distant riders, it had turned and disappeared within the doorway.

The maid's face brightened, as she met Weldon at the door. "But Mrs. Dent is not at home," she said, with honest regret in her voice. "She has gone out of town."

Weldon controlled his own voice as best he might.

"And Miss Dent?" he asked.

However, the maid had just broken the Baden-Powell tea-cup. Its fragments were still upon the floor, and she had no mind, just then, to face her young mistress.

"Miss Dent is not at home," she answered, with glib mendacity. And then she wondered why it was that Weldon's pallor turned from white to gray, as he went away down the steps.

Nevertheless, he fulfilled his resolution of going to the reception at the Citadel. For one reason, he had given his word to Carew. Moreover, he felt that, for the honor of his manhood, he must accept his fate like a man. Four months before that time, Ethel Dent had stabbed him almost to the death. Now, with delicate precision, she had struck him full across the face. The touch had hurt him far more than the deeper wound had done; but, at least, she should never be aware of it. To his mind, she had forfeited all right to the knowledge.

He dressed with careful precision. More than once he was forced to sit down for a moment; more than once his fingers refused to do his bidding and his hands dropped inertly at his side. However, Carew found him waiting, hat in hand, and together they drove away to the Citadel.

Already, when they reached the door, the reception was nearing its highest tide. The rooms were bright with uniforms and with trailing gowns, gay with the hum of voices; and the lilt of a waltz came softly to them from across the distance. As they halted on the threshold, Weldon lifted his eyes and suddenly found them resting full upon Ethel Dent. The girl was quite at the farther end of the long room, the central figure of a little throng, and wholly unconscious of their presence. Her back was towards Weldon. He could only see the sweep of her shimmering gown, the heavy coils of yellow hair and the curve of one rounding cheek; yet, even in that partial view, he felt himself astounded at her vitality. It flashed until it dazzled him, and the dazzle hurt. He bowed to the governor and turned away into another room, striving, as he went, to account for the sudden depression which had fallen upon him. He had not expected to find Ethel Dent moping alone in a corner; neither had he looked for a radiant alertness such as he had never seen in her before. During the long weeks of his illness, his mental picture of her had been colored by the sadness of their last meeting. Now the picture was torn aside and a new one thrust into its place, and the new one seemed garish to his weary nerves.

"Weldon! Have you risen from the grave?"

He turned sharply, to find himself face to face with the captain of his former troop.

"Merely from hospital," he answered. "I have been lying up for repairs."

The other man nodded.

"I know; and thereby adding to the glamour which surrounds a man elect for the V. C. Are you all right again?"

Weldon's voice hardened to match the strain he was putting upon his control.

"Absolutely. I am sailing for home, next week."

"And taking a farewell view of the place, before you go? Then come to meet the prettiest girl in Cape Town."

For an instant, Weldon hesitated. Then, reassured by the direction taken by his guide, he followed, while the strains of the waltz came ever more distinctly to his ears. His companion craned his neck to reconnoitre.

"She is dancing now; but she will be through in a moment. There," he added, as the music rose to a crashing finale; "that is over, and, by George, here she is! Miss Dent, may I introduce another war-worn veteran, Mr. Weldon?"

The shock came so suddenly that neither of them had an opportunity to prepare to resist it. It was Weldon who spoke first, however, and his voice was level, for he was generous enough to take none of the advantage which so plainly was all upon his side.

"Miss Dent and I are old acquaintances," he said quietly.

Fortunately the captain was garrulous.

"Another proof of the smallness of the world," he said jovially. "In time, I shall learn the futility of introductions. One is always pointing out next-door neighbors to each other's notice. By the way, Weldon, didn't you know Frazer rather well? I used to meet him at your house so often, Miss Dent."

Ethel's fingers shut upon the sticks of her fan.

"Yes," she assented. "Captain Frazer was one of our best friends."

All at once, the face of the young captain grew grave.

"I remember now," he said quite slowly. "But his loss was a sorrow to us all. His place can never be entirely filled."

There came a momentary pause. Then, as the captain's broad shoulders vanished in the heart of the crowd, Weldon turned and looked Ethel squarely between the eyes.

"Believe me, Miss Dent," he said simply; "this is none of my doing."

She made no pretence of misunderstanding him. Instead of that, her quiet voice was full of bitterness, as she gave brief answer,-- "Quite obviously, Mr. Weldon."

"Thank you for doing me that justice," he said, after an instant when their meeting eyes flashed like meeting blades of steel. "Stuart had no notion that he was making a mess of things."

She faced him a little proudly.

"I am unable to see what mess he can have made, Mr. Weldon. It is always a pleasure to meet an old acquaintance."

Few things could have hurt him more than the icy conventionality of her words. All the gentler side of his nature was crying out for mercy; but he smothered its cries and faced her bravely, praying the while for some one to come to them and end the scene. The Ethel Dent he had known in the old days had been a woman of flesh and blood; this was a statue of marble, polished and beautiful, but cold withal. He could only seek to meet her with equal coldness, then make his escape to nurse his wounds unseen. Nevertheless, in spite of his resolutions to the contrary, a sudden heat crept into his answering words,

"But I thought you had annulled the acquaintance."

She looked up at him in mute surprise. Then, mustering her pride, she forced herself to smile.

"I?" she answered lightly. "Oh, no, I am only too proud to count a V. C. among my friends."

He waited until the last word had dropped from her lips, waited until the silence had dropped over the last word. Then he faced her yet once again. This time, there was determination in his eyes, determination and a great, indomitable love.

"Ethel," he said imperiously; "for God's sake, stop fencing with me, and have it out. Remember it is now, or never."

The color mounted swiftly across her face, then faded, and even to her own ears her laugh failed to ring true.

"I am sorry; but I fear it is impossible. Here comes Colonel Andersen for his dance."

Weldon faced about.

"Colonel Andersen, Miss Dent is longing for an ice," he said, with a sudden masterful quietness. "May I take a convalescent's privilege and ask you to bring it to her?" Then he turned back to Ethel. "Come," he bade her.

"Where?" she protested; but she yielded to his stronger will and followed him across the floor towards a deserted corner of the room.

"Anywhere, where we can talk for a moment," he answered her, with the same dominant quietness. Then, while they halted beside an open window, he bent forward and laid his hand upon hers, as it rested upon the sill. "Ethel," he added; "I am going home, next week. I may never see South Africa again. Before I go--"

Quietly she withdrew her hand. "Before you go, you will come to say good by to my mother, I hope," she said, with a steadiness which gave no hint of the tears behind her lowered lids.

Impatiently he brushed her words aside.

"That is for you to say. First of all, I must know one thing."

Her nerve was failing fast; but she still held to her resolve that he should gain no hint of her weakness. She drew back a step, as if his vehemence terrified her, yet she dared not raise her eyes to his. It was all she could do to hold her voice in subjection.

"And what is that?" she asked.

He waited for an instant, before he answered her question. Her next words might contain all, or nothing. His lips shut to a narrow line; then he straightened his shoulders.

"Ethel," he said rapidly; "I have been in a good many fights; I've found that it hurts more to be mangled than it does to be killed. Speak out, then, and end this thing once for all. Was it final, what you said to the Captain, that day?"

She bit her lip; but her voice would not come, and she could only give a little, dreary nod. Weldon watched her steadily for a moment; then he turned to go away.

For another moment, Ethel stared after him, heedless now of the drops that were sliding down her cheeks. Then, of a sudden, she found her voice. "Wait!" she said, as she stepped forward with a swift gesture which was wholly imploring, wholly feminine. "It may have been final; but finality is not always truth."

He halted at her words.

"And you mean?"

"I mean," she answered him; "I mean that then, and now, and always, I loved one man, and he--" she caught her breath; then she lifted her head proudly; "was you. The rest was all a mistake; but I did what I thought was best."

Weldon bowed his head.

"No matter now," he answered.

Then, taking her hand, he led her back to the open window where they stood together long, while, in the room beyond, an anxious colonel threaded his way to and fro in the crowd, impatiently hunting the partner in whose memory he had ceased to exist.

THE END

www.ingramcontent.com/pod-product-compliance
Lightning Source LLC
Chambersburg PA
CBHW060506290526
45791CB00001B/295